Hoppla, We're Alive!
Ernst Toller

HOPPLA WE'RE ALIVE!

By Ernst Toller

Reconstructed, translated, and adapted by Drew Lichtenberg

New York and Berlin, 2023

Hoppla, We're Alive!
Drama by Ernst Toller
Translated from the German by Drew Lichtenberg
Editor: Eva C. Schweitzer
Proofreader: Lia Rockey
This printed edition Copyright © 2023

Berlinica Publishing LLC
255 West 43rd St., Suite 1012
New York, NY, 10036, USA

ISBN USA: 978-1-935902-49-2
Germany: 978-3-96026-042-4
LCCN: 2022950889
ISNI; 0000 0001 0884 6199

Cover: Eva C. Schweitzer

www.berlinica.com
blog.berlinica.com

Hoppla, We're Alive! by Ernst Toller is the second book in a new series of German and Austrian plays in translation presented by Berlinica Publishing. The series will present Weimar authors such as Bert Brecht, Kurt Tucholsky, Karl Kraus, and Walter Hasenclever, but also post-war authors like Rolf Hochhuth.

We would like to thank Dr. Dieter Distl, of the Toller-Archiv in Neuburg an der Donau, for his help and hospitality and also, the Ernst-Toller-Gesellschaft.

Dramatis Personae

In 1919:

Participants in the failed November Revolution of 1919:
  Karl Thomas
  Wilhelm Kilman
  Eva Berg
  Albert Kroll
  Mother Meller
  Prisoner 6

Rand, a prison warden
Baron Friedrich, a Lieutenant in the German Army

In 1927:

The former Revolutionaries:
  Karl Thomas, recently released from the insane asylum
  Wilhelm Kilman, Minister of the Interior, running for
  President of the Republic
  Eva Berg, Labor activist
  Albert Kroll, Election official for the
  German Communist Party
  Mother Meller, Waitress at the Grand Hotel
  Prisoner N

Rand, a Police Officer
Baron Friedrich

Characters from the 1927 world:
  Professor Lüdin, a State-appointed psychiatrist
  The Banker
  The Banker's Son
  Pickel, a private citizen from Holzhausen

Mrs. Kilman, Wilhelm Kilman's wife, late 30s
Lotte Kilman, Wilhelm Kilman's daughter, 18
Count Lande, leader of a paramilitary group
General von Landsring, Minister of Defense,
running for President of the Republic.
Fritz, Grete, Young people
Old Woman, a confused voter
Student, a right-wing terrorist
Telegram Operator, inventor of a device that could
feed all the hungry people in the world

Assorted Assistants, Secretaries, Guards, Policemen

Locations:

A prison
An insane asylum
The Ministry
An Election Hall
The Grand Hotel
A Police Station

This play is set in Berlin and many other places, during and eight years after the failure of an uprising of the people.

Prologue

Noise, Sirens, Searchlights
On the screen a film, showing a popular uprising... and its
failure. Characters from the prologue are emerging.

The Prison

A LARGE PRISON CELL, 1919.

KARL THOMAS: Damn this silence! It will drive me mad!

(*Silence*)

WILHELM KILMAN: Mother Meller, tell me. You're so quiet—Aren't you afraid? (*Moves close to her*) Please understand, Mother, I have a wife and child at home—I'm so afraid—

MOTHER MELLER: Hush, dear boy, you're just young. Someday you'll realize. Life, death, it all blurs together. We crawl out of the womb when we are born, we crawl toward our grave when we die.

(*Silence*)

EVA: They want to drive us mad.

MELLER: Yes, that's probably true.

THOMAS: Look. The window!

ALBERT: I'll be damned.

THOMAS: Don't you see? The caulk is crumbling.

EVA: It is!

MELLER: Yes. Truly.

KILMAN: What's the point? It will all be over soon.

ALBERT: Kilman, it's four in the morning. They've just changed the guard. If we stay here, we'll all be lying in a mass grave come morning. If we make a run for it, at least one of us has a chance of surviving. We have to take the risk.

KILMAN: But if we don't make it—

THOMAS: Then we're dead anyway. Let Eva go first. She's the youngest.

ALBERT: No. You have to go first, Karl, then you can catch Eva, then Wilhelm Kilman grabs Mother Meller and carries her—

KILMAN: Now wait a second—

MELLER: I don't need anyone's help. I'll take my chances with the rest of you.

KILMAN: We need a better plan.

THOMAS: You call yourself a revolutionary, and you won't take a risk like this? You were nowhere to be found when we were fighting on the barricades!

KILMAN: If all of us died fighting, who would be left to carry on the cause?

THOMAS: We've been waiting here for ten days, sentenced to death.

MELLER: Last night they asked for the names and addresses of our next of kin.

THOMAS: You speak of survival, where is the survival in that! We have a firing squad waiting for us outside that door. I'd rather die trying to survive than wait to be shot like a dog. (*KILMAN hangs his head.*) What are you going to do, ask them for mercy? If you're not going to help us, the least you can do is keep quiet. Don't ruin it for the rest of us.

KILMAN: You all stand silently and watch as he insults me! Haven't I worked by your sides, comrades, day and night? For fifteen years? I've been a loyal member of the party, and I should be allowed to have my say—

MELLER: Quiet, all of you!

THOMAS (*clasps KILMAN by the shoulder*): The state has ruled. Do you think they'll just forget about a death sentence?—What do you think it sounds like, when a man's body lands with a thud against a concrete wall?

ALBERT: Enough! Are we ready? Remember, Karl—on the count of five.

(*ALBERT KROLL begins to walk back and forth, from the door to the window, blocking the view of the warden from the keyhole. All of them are tense.*)

EVA: One—two—three— (*KARL THOMAS sneaks toward the window.*) Four—

(*A noise at the door. The door creaks open.*)

ALBERT: Damn it!

(*Enter WARDEN RAND*)

RAND: Does anyone wish to speak to the chaplain?

MELLER: You should be ashamed of yourself. Tell your chaplain that Jesus drove the money-changers from the Temple. Let him write that down in his Bible.

RAND: Don't add blasphemy to your crimes, old woman. You'll see your judge soon. (*To PRISONER 6, lying on a bench*) And you?

PRISONER 6 (*softly*): Please forgive me, comrades—I left the church when I was sixteen—but now—with death in front of me—it's so terrible to contemplate—please forgive me, comrades—

KILMAN: Go on, pissing and shitting like a baby! Go to the chaplain! (*Imitating him*) "Dear God, make me a pious man, so I can go to Heaven!"

MELLER: Will you leave that poor man alone?

ALBERT: It's a matter of life and death.

KILMAN: I'm just speaking my mind! (*Sits down and lights a cigarette with an ironic attitude.*)

(*RAND and PRISONER 6 exit. The door closes.*)

KILMAN: Do you think he'll betray us?

THOMAS: You would say that, wouldn't you, Kilman? You, you, you—bourgeois! (*Spits at him; KILMAN stands up, as if to fight.*)

ALBERT (*intervening*): Hey, Karl, forget about him! Now's the time! Warden Rand has to go with him, so he can't spy on us at. Come on, Karl, I'll help you. Here, climb on my back—!

(*KARL raises himself up on ALBERT's back. As he stretches his hands toward the window to grab the iron bars there is a rattle of gunfire from down below. KARL topples off ALBERT and both fall painfully to the ground. The prisoners stare at one another.*)

THOMAS: What was that?

ALBERT: They must be watching us from outside.

KILMAN: I told you it was no use.

EVA: Then that means—?

MELLER: Prepare yourself, my child.

EVA: But—Mother—I'm not ready to die!

(*The rest are silent as EVA sobs and says "No—no—" MOTHER MELLER goes and caresses her.*)

ALBERT: Don't cry, girl. Rosa Luxemburg didn't cry, Eva, when they bashed her head in with a rifle butt.

KILMAN: Didn't stop them from shooting her in the back and dumping her in the Landwehr Canal.

ALBERT: The mark of a true revolutionary is the willingness to die for a cause. She was richer in her death than you'll ever be in life, Kilman.

THOMAS (*crosses to EVA*): I love you very much, Eva.

EVA: Karl, do you think they'll bury us in the same grave?

THOMAS: Perhaps. It will be unmarked, though.

ALBERT (*jumps up*): God damn this torture! Why won't they come! These dogs! Ever since I was six years old, when I was thrown out of bed at five in the morning and forced to deliver hotcakes, I knew that society lived by the sweat of our hands. Before I could count to ten, I knew that we needed to fight like hell.

THOMAS: What makes people devote everything to an idea, to revolution, in times of war? There's only a few, at any given time—willing to do what must be done.

(*The door shrieks open. Enter PRISONER 6. Silence*)

PRISONER 6 (*looking guilty*): Can you blame me, comrades? I haven't converted—but—it gives one peace—

(*Silence*)

ALBERT: Still, nothing! Still, we wait! Does anyone have a cigarette? (*They search their pockets.*)

THOMAS: I do.

ALBERT: Matches?

KILMAN: I have one left.

ALBERT: We'll have to share it, obviously.

KILMAN: Really?

THOMAS: Eva can have my share.

MELLER: Mine too.

EVA: No, everyone takes a drag.

MELLER: Very well, then (*smokes*). Your turn, Kilman (*gives cigarette to WILHELM*).

KILMAN: Let's hope this doesn't get us in trouble.

ALBERT: What could they possibly do to us? Four more weeks of solitary confinement? (*Everyone laughs. They each smoke, taking a drag, watching each other sharply.*) Karl, you took two.

THOMAS: Don't talk such shit.

KILMAN (*to ALBERT*): You took the longest drag, Albert.

ALBERT: You know what, Kilman? I'm sick of you. Where were you on the day it all went down? You didn't get your nice clean uniform dirty, not when we stormed the town hall—the enemy at our backs, a mass grave yawning before us—what hole did you crawl into?

KILMAN: I spoke to the masses from City Hall, didn't I?

ALBERT: Yes, you did. As soon as we took power. After we did all the dirty work, you were on our side. But before that you were nowhere to be found. You maintained a pose of careful neutrality, watching which way the wind would blow. And then up you jumped, belly up to the feeding trough just like all the other pigs.

MELLER: Look at us, squabbling with each other, five minutes before we're going to be lined up against the wall and shot—

ALBERT: I think you should know, Kilman: I'm proud to die for the cause. But I consider it no great honor that I'll have to die standing next to you.

EVA: Now you're just being mean, Albert!

ALBERT: Oh, is little princess Eva upset! Karl, go lie in the corner with your whore, I'm sick of her, too—

(*EVA screams. KARL jumps at ALBERT, they grab each other by the throat.*)

PRISONER 6 (*praying*): Heavenly Father, is this thy will?

(*Noises. The door shrieks open. They let go of each other.*)

RAND: The Lieutenant is coming. Prepare yourselves to die (*goes*).

ALBERT (*goes to KARL THOMAS and embraces him*): I'm sorry, Karl. That wasn't me just now. Eva, please. I didn't mean it. I'm not myself at the moment.

THOMAS: We've been waiting around to die for ten days. They've slowly poisoned us against each other.

(*The door shrieks open. Enter BARON FRIEDRICH with SOL-DIERS.*)

BARON FRIEDRICH (*to ALBERT*): Stand up. As you know, you have all been sentenced to death, in full accordance with the law. (*Pause, disgusted*) As a sign of his graciousness and desire for reconciliation, the President of the Republic has issued a pardon. You will remain, for the time being, "alive." You are, however, to be kept in protective custody and transferred to the internment camp.

(*KARL THOMAS suddenly shrieks with laughter.*)

EVA: Karl, your laugh scares me.

BARON (*an order*): Stop laughing!

EVA (*shaking him*): Karl! Karl!

MELLER: He's gone mad.

BARON (*to RAND*): Take him to the doctor. (*RAND drags out KARL THOMAS, who is convulsed with laughter.*)

MELLER: Who could have thought that such a fine man could be so frail?

ALBERT: Who could have thought that he could be so strong?

BARON: The rest of you can go. Except for Kilman. He's going to stay here.

ALBERT (*as they leave, offers his hand to KILMAN*): Forgive me, Kilman, I was wrong about you. I'll never forget your sacrifice.

KILMAN (*looks at him meaningfully.*)

(*ALL leave except KILMAN.*)

BARON: Kilman, the President believes your story, that you found yourself among these rats against your will. You are free to come with us. He'd like to speak to you about forming a new government.

KILMAN: Thank you, Herr Lieutenant. I will always be in your debt.

(Curtain)

Filmic Interlude

At the rear of the stage:	On the SCREEN:
CHORUS (*swelling and ebbing, rhythmically*):	SCENES FROM 1919-1927
Happy New Year! Happy New Year!	1919: TREATY OF VERSAILLES
	1920: STOCK EXCHANGE RIOTS IN NEW YORK
Extra! Extra! Read all about it! Great sensation!	1921: FASCISM IN ITALY
Read all about it!	1922: HUNGER IN VIENNA
	1923: INFLATION IN GERMANY
In the middle-ground:	1924: LENIN'S DEATH IN RUSSIA
KARL THOMAS *walking back and forth in a madhouse in a hospital gown.*	1925: GANDHI IN INDIA
	1926: RIOTS IN CHINA. MEETING OF EUROPEAN HEADS OF STATE
Noise: Clocks	1927: A CLOCKFACE, THE HANDS MOVING, FIRST SLOWLY... THEN FASTER AND FASTER...

ACT ONE

Scene One. The Madhouse

MADHOUSE. EXAMINATION ROOM, 1927.

KARL THOMAS is being examined, physically and mentally, by ATTENDANT. PROFESSOR LÜDIN stands behind a barred window, holding a clipboard.

ATTENDANT (*making notes*): One pair: gray slacks. One pair: wool socks. No underwear?

THOMAS (*blankly*): I can't remember.

ATTENDANT: Jacket: one, black. One pair: military boots. (*Checking them off, comes to the end of his list.*) And no hat! Perfect.

PROFESSOR: Any money?

ATTENDANT: None, doctor.

PROFESSOR: Living relatives?

THOMAS (*numb*): I learned yesterday that my mother died three years ago.

PROFESSOR: Then it will be hard for you, I'm afraid. Life is hard these days, Mr. Thomas.

ATTENDANT: Release date: November 9, 1927.

THOMAS: What? November 9! That can't be possible!

PROFESSOR: But it is.

THOMAS: What year is it? 1927?

PROFESSOR: What did you expect, Karl Thomas? You've been a ward of the state for eight years. All this time, the taxpayers have been bathing you, clothing you, feeding you, even paying for you to shit—for eight years! No expense spared. Did you expect that we would pay for you forever?

THOMAS: It's as if the past—everything we've fought for—has been murdered, extinguished—or worse, committed suicide. But I remember...

PROFESSOR: You remember what?

THOMAS: I remember—I remember standing, at the edge of a forest, a forest of beech trees. All white. Trunks rising to the heavens. A whole forest flickering green, with the light of a thousand little suns. I wanted to go for a walk—to experience freedom—but I couldn't. The tree-trunks threw me back, I bounced off them like a rubber ball. And then I woke up and found myself here—inside these rubber walls. On November 9.

PROFESSOR: Hmm. Rubber ball. Very interesting. Think of it this way: your forest is your padded cell. Your tree trunks are rubber walls of the highest quality, preventing you from harming yourself. Once a year, every November, you would start to rage, out of control. You had to be placed there, for your own safety. And always on the same exact day. Truly, a remarkable case!

THOMAS: On which day?

PROFESSOR: November 9.

The projections on the screen:
Images of November 9 throughout German history.

Images of 1919: *Kaiser Wilhelm II abdicating... Karl Liebknecht proclaiming a Free Socialist Republic from the balcony of the Berlin City Palace... and the resulting fighting in the streets.*

Images of 1923: *Hitler's Beer Hall Putsch... a coup in the streets of Munich... Hitler writing* Mein Kampf *in prison.*

Images of 1938: *Kristallnacht... burning synagogues and looted Jewish businesses... thousands of Jews deported to concentration camps.*

Images of 1989: *The fall of the Berlin Wall*

THOMAS (*speaks as the images play*): The day I was to be executed, and then pardoned—the day of so many horrible events, sights impossible to describe. I remember—waiting for death, for ten days—every hour: sixty minutes. Every minute: sixty seconds. Every second: a death. Murdered: 1,440 times a day!—I wished I was dead. That I could end it somehow. I hate the President, for pardoning me. If I could be alone in a room with him, I'd show him what I think of his "Republic"!

PROFESSOR: Easy now, easy. You should be thanking your friends in high places, Karl Thomas. In here, we don't take such words seriously. But outside—you could spend the rest of your life in here, sucking on the taxpayers' teat.

THOMAS: I've had all I can stomach, thank you.

PROFESSOR: There's no shame in having been institutionalized, you know. Some of our finest citizens have spent time in here. And many thousands who would benefit from it. If I could administer just a few of my finest psychotropic drugs to the average civilian, I think I could make a good deal of change in the world.

THOMAS: You're a sick man.

PROFESSOR (*not listening*): Someday, soon, the state will see the wisdom of my ways. But I hope you've gotten over your madness, Karl Thomas—a social reformer! Ha! I hope you don't do anything foolish when you're discharged. You should go stay with a friend.

THOMAS: There were only five of us, a little group. We all got pardoned, except for the only one willing to die for their beliefs—Wilhelm Kilman.

PROFESSOR: Wilhelm Kilman! Not pardoned? (*Laughs*) You're funny.

THOMAS: I don't understand.

PROFESSOR: You'll see soon enough. Maybe you should go stay with him! (*Laughs*) If he wants to remember who you are, that is.

THOMAS: Kilman is still alive?

PROFESSOR: Miracles still happen, my friend. You should go see him. Clinically speaking, you're cured. But only he can cure you of your crazy ideas. Go to the Ministry of the Interior and ask for Mr. Kilman. Good luck!

THOMAS: Okay. Goodbye, Doctor.—That's strange. It smells of lilacs in here—of course. Outside the window. Real beech trees—not rubber walls— (*exits*).

PROFESSOR: Inferior stock! He'll be back in here in no time.

(*Blackout*)

FILMIC INTERLUDE

THE CITY IN 1927
STREETCARS, AUTOMOBILES
SUBWAYS, AIRPLANES
POTSDAMER PLATZ

[*For hints of a stylistic comparison, see: Walter Ruttman's 1927 film,* Berlin: Sinfonie einer Großstadt]

Scene Two. The Ministry

Interior: two rooms in the Reichstag. Wilhelm Kilman's Office at the Ministry of the Interior and the waiting-room outside.

OFFICE

KILMAN: I sent for you.

EVA: And here I am.

WAITING ROOM

BANKER'S SON: He didn't send for us, father.

BANKER: He wouldn't dare turn us away!

SON: We need a line of credit to make it to the end of the month. He's already rejected you twice.

BANKER: I put it clumsily to him before. Besides, what's he going to do? If he doesn't keep the biggest bank in Berlin solvent, the whole economy might collapse!

OFFICE

KILMAN: Hello, Eva.

EVA: Hello, Minister.

KILMAN: Still a thorn in my side, I see.

EVA: I remember what we once fought for. Unlike you.

KILMAN: You represent the Women's Workers Union, yes?

EVA: Yes.

KILMAN: And at the same time you work as secretary in the Ministry of Finance?

EVA: Yes.

KILMAN: Seems like a conflict of interest, no? (*No response from EVA.*) Your name has been popping up in police reports recently.

EVA: I don't follow.

KILMAN: Why have you been telling the women at the chemical factories to demand overtime? Don't you realize that I have factory owners who aren't happy with me?

EVA: I am merely encouraging them to exercise their constitutional rights.

KILMAN: The constitution was intended for times of peace and quiet.

EVA: Don't we live in those now?

KILMAN: There's the trick: there is never truly a time of peace and quiet.

WAITING ROOM

BANKER: The matter needs to be regulated before the trade deal goes through. We have two more hours.

SON: The unions are demanding overtime plus an eight-hour work day. We'll have to lock out a million workers if you don't agree!

BANKER: Kill two birds with one stone. Find workers to replace them, then we can institute longer hours and lower wages. Besides, whatever is good for the economy is good for us.

OFFICE

EVA: What are you making in those factories anyway? Poison gas!

KILMAN (*changing the subject*): Are you the author of this pamphlet?

EVA: Yes.

KILMAN: It's illegal for an elected official to be distributing activist literature. You're in breach of your duties.

EVA: There was a time you would have done the same.

KILMAN: That's conjecture. Need I remind you that we are having an official conversation, Ms. Berg?

EVA: There was a time when you would have—

KILMAN: Let's stick to the present, shall we? Please try to be reasonable. I don't want anything bad to happen to you and, in any case, you lack the necessary qualifications, the practical knowledge to bring all the factories in Germany to a standstill. It would be very uncomfortable—for us both—if I had to go against you. I remember you fondly from the old days, but I would be forced to—do you see what I'm saying?

EVA: Are you threatening me, Minister Kilman?

KILMAN (*getting agitated*): Not at all. I'm only trying to help you—to warn you. If you do this, you alone will bear the responsibility.

EVA: I'm willing to fight for what I believe in.

KILMAN: Look, I'm just saying, we should both try be reasonable. Can you promise me that?

EVA: I promise nothing. (*EVA goes*)

KILMAN (*thinks for a second, then picks up the telephone*): Chemical factory?—Kilman here.

WAITING ROOM

PICKEL (*who has been pacing back and forth, stops in front of the BANKERS*): Excuse me, my good Sirs… I am a private citizen, from Holzhausen. Perhaps you fine gentlemen know of Holzhausen? It's in the municipality of Münsing, which is in the district of Bad Tölz-Wolfratshausen, which is bounded by Garmisch-Partenkirchen and Weilheim-Schongau. The construction of the railway line to Holzhausen is scheduled to begin in October, but I took the mail-coach here and it was more than sufficient. Although a bit bumpy, as we say in Holzhausen…

GENERAL VON LANDSRING (*entering, interrupting PICKEL*): Ah, good morning, Director. You're here as well?

BANKER: Yes. Allow me to introduce my son. This is General von Landsring, the Minister of Defense.

GENERAL: The pleasure is mine. (*Shakes hands.*) Tricky business, this "peacetime," isn't it, Director? (*PICKEL, being ignored, goes to the corner, rummages in his pocket, and digs out a medal, which he struggles to pin to himself as the others are talking*) It's not exactly any fun, is it? To be forbidden from shooting people? It's like giving someone sticks and then telling them not to beat the drums! This Kilman and his liberal utopia of "democracy" and "freedom"—it's never going to work. What will happen to our history? To thousands of years of authority? You can't just shout that down with fancy slogans.

BANKER: Well, General, democracy might be slower and more bureaucratic than other ways of running a country, but at least it serves as a safety valve, as a check on the baser instincts of—

GENERAL: Democracy! Government by the people! Nonsense. I suppose you also think it's a good thing that women now have the right to vote, do you? Let's not mince words here, Director, I'll tell you what I prefer—

(*enter COUNT LANDE*)

COUNT: General!

GENERAL: Ah, Count Lande. How are things among our friends in the country?

COUNT: Armed and ready, just waiting for the signal, General! You give the word and they'll be in the streets of Berlin the next day.

GENERAL: Now don't get too hot-headed, Count. We don't need foolish talk of military strikes. For the moment, anything we want for the Fatherland must be obtained through legal means.

COUNT: We await your command, Sir.

GENERAL: My dear Count. With all due sympathy—I'm warning you. (*Clasps him on the shoulder and goes.*)

PICKEL (*to LANDE*): Excuse me, Sir, I'm a private citizen, from Holzhausen. It's in the municipality of Münsing. (*Waits for a response, but gets only blank stares*) Do you know when Minister Kilman will see me? I was hoping to speak with him at noon and it's already quarter past twelve! (*PICKEL turns his attention to his watch, which he winds and holds up to his ear*)

BANKER: The idiot has a point. How long is Kilman going to make us wait?

SON: Why don't we just do our business with Count Lande and General von Landsring? We could throw this Kilman and his democracy out the window. Move faster, break a few eggs, upset the apple cart, and make billions of dollars. This democracy is too slow, too inefficient. One step forward and two steps back.

BANKER: Kilman is in power at the moment. Better safe than sorry. You never know when you're going to need a friend.

SON: He's passé. Besides, what's wrong with nationalism? Don't you love your country? You can tell which way the industrial winds are blowing, father. I'd bet by this time next year this country will be a dictatorship.

PICKEL (*turning to LANDE*): Could you tell me the time, Sir?

COUNT: Quarter past twelve.

PICKEL (*winding his watch again*): The clocks in the city always run so fast. I hoped for an audience with the Minister at noon sharp!... Though I must admit the clocks in the country always run slow, as a result... (*continues to pace up and down.*)

(*Enter BARON FRIEDRICH*)

COUNT: Ah, Baron Friedrich!

BARON: Count Lande.

COUNT: Tell me, Baron, what do you think of Kilman, making us wait out here like dogs?

BARON: It's an old story. Put a man in uniform, and soon he's acting the part.

COUNT: Ten years ago, I wouldn't have spit on him in the street!

BARON: I can tell you something, Count. Eight years ago, I nearly had him lined up against the wall and shot.

COUNT: Now that is fabulously interesting. You were there? You saw this?

BARON: I'd prefer not to discuss the details.

COUNT: And yet he installed you in his cabinet anyway. He always keeps you close by. You must have done a number on his nerves.

BARON (*laughs*): Yes. When he came into the Ministry, everyone made great airs about him. He looked me up and down, sharply. And from that day, one promotion has followed another. And he has never said a word of his revolutionary past.

COUNT: One can never be sure how times will change, especially with all this—economic anxiety.

BARON: Indeed.

COUNT: How does he keep his past secret?

BARON: I don't know. He's clever, this Kilman: I don't know if he took acting lessons, but to look at him now you'd say he's a pure aristocrat, from head to toe.

COUNT: They have imitated us in everything.

BARON: Satin shoes, single-breasted lounge coat, starched collar and bowler: he cuts quite the fashionable figure. (*Projection: images of Gustav Stresemann in his signature suit.*)

PICKEL (*interjecting*): You know, my neighbor in Holzhausen told me about this! "Pickel!" he said. "You must buy white gloves for your audience with the Minister. That's always the way it was in the old days, and that's the way it still remains." I thought things would be different... during the monarchy, everyone wore white gloves... now, everyone's still wearing white gloves! It's the same thing, not even a different color. Back then, supposedly, we were slaves. Today, supposedly, we're free men. Ha! (*Goes back to pacing up and down.*)

COUNT (*as he watches PICKEL*): The pig can dress up all he wants to, his butthole still reeks of the proletariat.

BARON: Yes, every inch. There's just something—off about him. In every word, every gesture—(*leans in, confidentially*): I've heard rumors that he's secretly a Jew.

OFFICE

SECRETARY: Sir, your wife and daughter are waiting in the parlor.

KILMAN: I'll see them in ten minutes. (*SECRETARY exits. Telephone rings*) "Hello. Ah, Counselor. Yes, it's me… about this strike at the chemical factory… I can assure you that everything will be fine, despite what the newspapers say. Yes, the funds for the deal with Turkey were approved yesterday—unanimously—three per-cent—Goodbye." (*Hangs up.*)

SECRETARY (*enters*): Sir, the ladies—

KILMAN: Tell them to wait! I'm working.

WAITING ROOM

(*FRIEDRICH and LANDE are laughing at a dirty joke somebody has just told.*)

COUNT: Hahahaha.—Ahhhh… sitting around in the capital is like waiting to lose one's virginity. Governing doesn't come very easily to him, does it?

(*KARL THOMAS enters. Sits in the corner.*)

SECRETARY (*enters, to LANDE and FRIEDRICH*): The Prime Minister will see you now...

BANKER: Excuse me, but I have an appointment too. (*Shows his card to SECRETARY and forces his way into Kilman's office with SON.*)

OFFICE

KILMAN: Ah, good morning, Director! I'm afraid my schedule today is quite full—

BANKER: Should we meet this evening, perhaps, at the Grand Hotel?

KILMAN: Sounds good. See you then. (*BANKER and SON exit.*)

ANTECHAMBER

SECRETARY (*to LANDE and FRIEDRICH*): The Minister begs your pardon.

(*He opens the door to the office. LANDE and FRIEDRICH go in. SECRETARY is about to exit.*)

THOMAS: Excuse me!

SECRETARY: The Minister's schedule is very busy today. He doesn't have time to see any other visitors today.

THOMAS: I don't want to speak with the Minister. I want to see Wilhelm Kilman.

SECRETARY: Try out your jokes on someone else.

THOMAS: Jokes, comrade?

SECRETARY: I'm not your comrade.

THOMAS: Wilhelm Kilman works here, doesn't he? When I asked at the desk for Mr. Kilman, I was sent here.

SECRETARY: Where have you been the last eight years? Are you trying to tell me that you don't know that Wilhelm Kilman is the Minister of the Interior, the most powerful economic official in the country?

THOMAS: Surely you must mean a different Kilman? There are many Kilman—

SECRETARY: Look. What do you want?

THOMAS: I would like to talk to Mr. Wilhelm Kilman. Kilman: K-I-L-M-A-N.

SECRETARY: I know how the Minister spells his name. (*Gets up.*)

THOMAS: Kilman the Minister?—No, stay! I mean, I know him! Very well. In fact, I'm his friend. Eight years ago, we were—

SECRETARY: We don't talk about those times here.

THOMAS: Please, please stay for a second. Do you have a paper and pencil? I'll write my name down; I'm sure he'll receive me at once. (*SECRETARY is unsure*) Come on, man!

SECRETARY: One can't be too careful these days, with all the psychos running around. (*Gives KARL THOMAS paper and pen. Leaves. KARL THOMAS writes.*)

PICKEL: So, you are a friend of the Prime Minister. My name is Pickel, I am a citizen from Holzhausen, which is south of Reichenkam and north of Weidenkam, in Münsing. That assistant—so rude! You know, we have to deal with everything, everyone being "equal" these days, it seems that guys like us are always stuck waiting out here in the corridor. One ought to be allowed to spend five minutes speaking with the man you've voted to elect. I mean, something ought to be done. It's a flaw in the republic...

OFFICE

KILMAN (*in mid-conversation*): You see, gentlemen, democracy is a delicate thing. One must know how to handle the masses, tell them what they want to hear, not dictate to them. Every foreign Minister worth their salt bleats about "world peace" and "humanitarianism," but I guarantee you every one of them sets aside money for poison gas and arms.

COUNT: Maybe that's why they think so highly of you in nationalist circles.

KILMAN (*not listening*): Slander from the left—slander from the right—both sides.

BARON: And this tariff business, surely you don't mean to make a deal with—

KILMAN: You shouldn't worry about things you don't understand, Friedrich.

SECRETARY (*enters*): Excuse me, Sir, your wife and daughter—

KILMAN: Show them in. (*Enter MRS. and LOTTE KILMAN*) My dear, you know Baron Friedrich—

BARON (*kisses MRS. KILMAN's hand*): My dear lady.

KILMAN: Count Lande: my daughter, Lotte.

COUNT: Of course, the beautiful Lotte. (*Kisses her hand*) Mademoiselle.

MRS. KILMAN: Baron Friedrich, I just wrote, inviting you to dinner on Sunday.

BARON: I'd love to be your guest.

MRS. KILMAN: Perhaps you can bring your handsome friend along with you.

COUNT: Too honored, my lady.

LOTTE (*aside, to BARON FRIEDRICH*): Hey, you abandoned me in the park yesterday.

BARON (*aside*): Dear girl, I'll make it up to you.

LOTTE: Your friend looks interesting. Maybe I'll trade you in for him.

BARON: Lucky for him.

LOTTE: I've heard his speeches on the radio. Shocking.

BARON: When will I see you again?

WAITING ROOM

THOMAS (*pacing back and forth*): Minister Kilman—Minister Kilman!

PICKEL (*pacing in the opposite direction*): It's not fair! I was waiting here first. And I've come all the way from Holzhausen!

(*LANDE and BARON FRIEDRICH pass through.*)

BARON (*claps him on the shoulder*): See, Count, what did I tell you?

COUNT: Maybe democracy has its uses, after all. (*BOTH exit*)

THOMAS (*watching them go, stares at FRIEDRICH's face*): I've seen that face before. But where?

PICKEL: Friendship goes ahead of democracy.

(*Enter SECRETARY*)

THOMAS: Ah! There you are. Here is my letter for the Minister (*SECRETARY looks at him, takes the letter, and exits into the Minister's Office*).

OFFICE

SECRETARY: There is a man here to see you, Sir.

KILMAN: I told you, I don't have time—

THOMAS (*knocks on the door, enters without waiting for an answer*): Wilhelm! Wilhelm!

KILMAN: Who are you?

THOMAS: You don't recognize me, do you? After all eight years—

KILMAN (*turns pale; to SECRETARY*): You can go. Go! Now! (*SECRETARY exits.*)

THOMAS: You're still alive! It's a miracle! But tell me—we were all pardoned, except you.

KILMAN (*looks ashamed*): A lucky coincidence.

THOMAS: Eight years—buried, as if in the grave. Oh, Wilhelm. I told the doctors I remembered nothing, but I saw your face every night in my sleep—I saw you—dead!—I dug my nails into my eyes until blood spurted out—the guards thought I was suffering seizures.

KILMAN: That's funny. I don't think too much about those days. I don't like to remember them.

THOMAS: Death loomed over us. Pitted us against one another.

KILMAN: We were children.

THOMAS: The hours we spent together—don't you see? They bind us, stronger than blood. That's why I came here to see you, when I heard you were alive.

LOTTE: Who is this man?

MRS. KILMAN (*stiffens*): He's nobody. Wilhelm, we must go.

THOMAS: Mrs. Kilman. I didn't recognize you.—Do you remember, how you visited your husband in his prison cell? They had to drag you out. Hands over your face, you kept screaming, "No, no, no!"

MRS. KILMAN (*hesitates, and then*): Yes, I remember. It was a horrible time. Wasn't it, Wilhelm?

THOMAS: And you must be Lotte. How big you've grown!

LOTTE: Everyone grows up, sooner or later. My father is the Minister now. What are you?

THOMAS: I'm—I'm—

MRS. KILMAN (*changing the subject*): It's good to see you're doing well. How nice. You must drop by sometime.

THOMAS: I—thank you, Mrs. Kilman. I hope that I will. (*MRS. KILMAN and LOTTE go.*) Does she have to do that, your daughter? Dress like that?

KILMAN: What?

THOMAS: And this Ministry, this is all a trick, isn't it? Nothing more than a bluff? In the old times, we wouldn't have approved of such tactics. Working inside against the enemy. Is the whole state apparatus really in your hands? Have you really taken hold of the means of production?

KILMAN: You talk as if we were still little children, playing at being revolutionaries. Almost ten years have passed. All those illusions are gone. Where once we saw in straight lines, reality intruded, as it always does. There is still a path forward, though a crooked one.

THOMAS: Then you are really just an ordinary government Minister now? A member of a functioning democracy?

KILMAN: Of course I am. What did you think?

THOMAS: And what of the people?

KILMAN: I am their servant.

THOMAS: Didn't you once say to me never to trust someone who ends up becoming a Minister? That in order to attain such a position, he must betray his ideals, no matter his intentions? That he holds his mortal enemies closer than his best friends?

KILMAN: Life is not lived through theories. One must learn from experience.

THOMAS: Albert was right. They should have lined you up against that wall and shot you!

KILMAN: Still the hot-headed dreamer, I see. I'm not offended. We seek to govern in a democracy. And what is a democracy? The will of the people. All of the people. As an elected official, I can't represent any one party, only the state. If you had this kind of power, my friend, you might see things differently. One must ride power, it's like breaking in a horse.

THOMAS: Power! What good is it, imagining you have power, when the people have none! I've looked around for the last five days. Can you tell me what has changed? You sit up here, high in your fancy office, and oversee daily theft on a massive scale. Don't you see that you've abandoned your ideals, that you govern now against the people?

KILMAN: Sometimes it takes real courage to govern against the people. More courage than in manning barricades. (*Telephone rings.*) Excuse me. "Kilman here.—Unanimous, then, no overtime.—Thank you, Director.—Any names on the pamphlet?—Listen: whoever leaves the factory at five o'clock is to be replaced—well, the factories will have to close for a day or two, then, won't they? Yes, yes, I'll negotiate with the companies. The Turkish orders need to be fulfilled.—Goodbye, Director." (*Hangs up. Telephone rings again.*) "Contact the police, it's in relation to Eva Berg." (*Hangs up.*)

THOMAS: Such courage!

KILMAN: The mechanism of the state is complicated. And easily stained by dirty hands.

THOMAS: Aren't those women fighting for your ideals?

KILMAN: Should I disgrace myself? Show myself to be weak? It's not so easy—if you fail even once in this job, then—oh, what do you know?

THOMAS: How does it show any strength to beat up striking workers and cut deals for corporations?

KILMAN: In a democracy, I have to respect the rights of everybody, the employers as much as the workers.

THOMAS: But they have control of the press, they have all the money, they have weapons on their side. What do the workers have? Empty hands.

KILMAN: You always see things in terms of armed struggle! Onto the barricades, all you workers! We have rejected the politics of brute force. Violence will always be reactionary.

THOMAS: Oh, is that the opinion of the masses? Have you even asked them what they think?

KILMAN: What are the masses, anyway? Have they ever been capable of building anything positive? No! Proverbs and slogans! Smash and grab! We face a simple and inescapable choice: stability and strong government with me, or chaos with them.—Let's be honest, the masses are incompetent, and uneducated, and they always will be. People who have only ever known coffeehouse debate their whole lives. Do you want to know what I've done, Karl Thomas? (*Slams the table for emphasis.*) I have saved the revolution. How could a worker with no economic training take over the management of a corporation? Maybe some day—after decades—after centuries. But today—it is we who must govern.

THOMAS: To think I went to the wall with you—

KILMAN: You look at the world in a very simplistic way, Karl Thomas. To you, every rich man is a parasite, every illiterate worker a saint! If you could only comprehend what free-market capitalism has made possible.

THOMAS: What has it made possible, exactly? Look at our world! What has it become? If we could just push for something better—

KILMAN: It all depends on tactics, Karl. If we used yours, it would lead to the darkest of times.

THOMAS: These are the darkest of times, Kilman.

KILMAN: You are a dreamer. A foolish child.

THOMAS: And who do you think props you up? The aristocrats of the old regime? What have you become? Their puppet, a rubber ball for them to play with!

KILMAN: Better than a zombie that no one has any use for. What do you want? To see how it works? It runs like clockwork. Everyone here knows his business.

THOMAS: I suppose that makes you proud?

KILMAN: Yes, it does.

THOMAS: You said a name just now, on the telephone.

KILMAN: Matters of state.

THOMAS: Eva Berg. She must be older by now.

KILMAN: We're all older. Eight years older. She works at the Ministry of Finance now, and in her free time she's a constant thorn in my side. Maybe you should go talk to her, Mr. Thomas: I expect you would have a great deal to talk about.

THOMAS: What happened to the pretty girl we once knew?

KILMAN: I tried to spare her. Talk sense into her.—Well, this has been a lovely trip down memory lane, but I need to get back to business. Here, you could use this. (*Offers KARL THOMAS money; he refuses it.*) I can't give you a position here at the Ministry, I'm afraid. Go talk to Eva. Or maybe go to the unemployment office. You'll find some old comrades there, I suspect. One loses touch so easily these days… Good luck. And don't do anything foolish.

THOMAS: This isn't the end.

KILMAN: I hope it isn't. (*Pauses, then shakes hands with him.*)
We still have the same goal, you know. Just different means...

(*He shows KARL THOMAS into the waiting room gently.
KILMAN remains standing for a few moments.*)

ANTECHAMBER

(*KARL THOMAS enters and stares, silently.*)

PICKEL (*to SECRETARY*): Is it my turn now?

SECRETARY: Do you have an appointment?

PICKEL: I took the mail-train, from Holzhausen, for two and a
half days, Mr. Secretary!

SECRETARY: Why do you wish to speak to the Minister?

PICKEL: On account of the railroad planned for construction
in Holzhausen.

SECRETARY: Okay. I'll ask him. (*Exits into the Office.*)

PICKEL: Well would you look at that! The Minister is a very
great man, isn't he? (*KARL THOMAS doesn't answer.*) If
the Good Lord made a minister, he would look something
like him. (*PICKEL resumes his pacing.*)

OFFICE

KILMAN: Alright, show him in.

SECRETARY (*opens the door*): Mr. Pickel?

PICKEL (*enters*): Good day, Sir! Excuse me, Mr. Prime Minister, I must have been weighing heavily on your mind all morning. My name is Pickel: native of Holzhausen, which is just across Lake Starnberg from Tutzing! I have come on account of the railway, which is scheduled to be built, you see... this railway, well, it would run straight across my property, you see... I'm not keeping you, am I, Mr. Prime Minister?

KILMAN: Well, out with it. What do you have to say about the railroad?

PICKEL: I told my neighbors, that if I were to talk to you, Mr. Prime Minister, I mean, you must be so smart! You know so many things, whether there will be war, whether the railroad will pass over my property or not... (*gets another idea*) Um, if it's not asking too much, do you mind if I ask you... just... where you think all of this is going?... I mean, if you build a railroad through Holzhausen, then can you take it all the way around the world?... And, well, who makes money from all this, Mr. Prime Minister? They say that the government will get rid of all money one of these days... You sit there, and you have to deal with all of this... Do you ever ask yourself: What's going to become of the world?

KILMAN: What's going to become of the world?

PICKEL: Yes! What will come of it, Mr. Minister? I mean (*gestures wildly*) all of it!

KILMAN: What's going to become of the world... hmm... it's not so easy to answer that, Mr. Pickel.

(*A knock*)

SECRETARY: Sir, your next appointment—

KILMAN: My dear Mr. Pickel, take my advice. Go back to Holzhausen and try to make peace with all that's coming. The railroad, and someday the high-rise buildings, and after that, who knows? It's the future, you see, Mr. Pickel. It's inevitable. And give my best to everyone in Holzhausen.

PICKEL: Yes, Sir, Mr. Minister, Sir. But this railroad... Do you really have to send it through my property, can't you just...?

KILMAN (*pushes PICKEL gently into the Antechamber.*)

WAITING ROOM

PICKEL (*going out*): I guess I'll have to go back in Holzhausen.

SECRETARY (*to KARL THOMAS, who is still staring*): You must leave now. We are closing for the day.

ACT TWO

Scene One. Eva's Apartment

INTERIOR OF APARTMENT.

EVA BERG jumps out of bed and begins to dress. She is utterly unlike the 17-year-old in Act One but now a completely modern woman, busy, confidently sexual, unsentimental, politically pragmatic, and above all hardened by life.

THOMAS (*in bed*): Where are you going?

EVA: You're sweet. To work.

THOMAS: What time is it?

EVA: Six-thirty.

THOMAS: Stay here. It's not even eight o'clock. Your office hours don't start until nine.

EVA: I have to run down to the Union Hall. The election is only a week away and the pamphlets have been printed all wrong. I designed new ones last night while you were sleeping.

THOMAS: I get lazier every day.

EVA: Yes. It's time you found a job.

THOMAS (*looking at her hair*): What do you call that? A bob? How long have you been wearing your hair like that?

EVA (*touches her hair absentmindedly while focusing on her work*): Oh, you like it? It's terrible, they're still missing union reps for district six. (*She reads and corrects her papers.*)

THOMAS: It suits you. Your face is so beautiful.

EVA (*turning to ice*): Uh-huh.

THOMAS: I walk around and I see all these naked faces in the streets, in the subways—not hidden by hair. They're awful. I've never noticed before, how most faces are just lumps of flesh, bloated by fear, fat with food.

EVA (*looking at him now*): Tell me, Karl. Did you feel lust while you were inside?

THOMAS: I felt I was—buried alive, as if I was in the grave. I didn't feel a thing until the last year.

EVA: It must have been awful. (*Then, quickly*) You need to find work, Karl.

THOMAS: I don't care about work any more. Since my meeting with Kilman, I detest everything. Why should we kill ourselves, all so our old comrade can grin back at us in the mirror, like distorted images of the old world? No, Eva. I don't dream of revolution anymore. I dream of you. You are my dream of the future.

EVA: Stop.

THOMAS: I'm serious, Eva! Come away with me! We can travel. To Greece. To India. Africa. Somewhere there must be people who still live a life that is free, free from politics, free from this constant struggle!

EVA: So you want to flee?

THOMAS: Call it whatever you want. I don't care.

EVA: Do you really think that other people's lives are any more free than ours? You're deluding yourself, Karl. This paradise you dream of doesn't exist. And if we don't do something, we'll die in this city, like caged animals.

THOMAS (*soberly*): I guess you're right. (*Begins to get dressed.*)

EVA: You should find another place to stay.

THOMAS: Can't I stay here with you?

EVA: Honestly, no.

THOMAS: Is it the landlady?

EVA: I just have to live on my own. Please try to understand, Karl.

THOMAS: What is it, then? Don't you love me?

EVA: You think because I fucked you that I'm in love with you?

THOMAS: Doesn't that bind us together?

EVA: You still speak of great things binding us together, as if I was the foolish and idealistic girl I was eight years ago. But things have changed, Karl. A glance shared with a stranger on the street binds me more deeply than any night of love. This doesn't need to be anything more than what it is, Karl, a beautiful reunion. Think of it as a farewell and a burial at the same time.

THOMAS: Do you take anything seriously?

EVA: Oh, I do take it seriously. Don't misunderstand me. The notion that one must give up all of life's little joys because of one's politics is absurd. Everyone should be allowed to do whatever they want.

THOMAS: Is anything sacred to you?

EVA: Why use mystical words for objective things? Why are you staring at me?

THOMAS: Objective?

EVA: It's only been eight years but it might as well be a century.

THOMAS: Yes. Sometimes I think I come from a generation that has gone missing without a trace.

EVA: That was an unfortunate episode—

THOMAS: How can you speak like that about the revolution!

EVA: Because that's what it was. An episode. It is over.

THOMAS: And what remains?

EVA: The struggle. The desire for truth. To do new work.

THOMAS: And what if we were to have a child?

EVA: I won't bring a child into this world, Karl.

THOMAS: Is it because you don't love me anymore?

EVA: You're not even listening to me! Because it would be an accident. A mistake. Because it wouldn't be necessary.

THOMAS: Forgive me if I'm saying stupid things. Just know that I need you. I held you once, and I felt alive, even though we were surrounded by the sounds of death. And now I find myself alone, lost. Help me, please!

EVA: You're being silly. You feel—

THOMAS: I feel nothing.

EVA: You feel afraid. Of walking out that door and seeing what you might find.

THOMAS: Please don't say that.

EVA: No. You listen to me. You need to make a new beginning, Karl. Or you will fall to pieces.

THOMAS: Why are you so hard? What is it you have lived through that has made you like this?

EVA: I was a child back then. And we can no longer afford to be children. I have lived through a lot. Many men, many situations. For eight years I worked the way only men used to work. For eight years I decided how to spend my money, how to spend every free hour of my life. It wasn't easy for me. I remember sitting in one of these hideous rooms, throwing myself down on the bed and crying—howling—but it was the struggle, the struggle which always came first. The party needed me. Karl, please. Try to think clearly. I have to go. (*FRITZ and GRETE peep through the door, then vanish.*) You can spend the morning here, but that's all. Here, take some money.

THOMAS: First Kilman and now you. Why is it that everyone wants to give me money?

EVA: Take it. Don't say no out of some stupid sense of honor. I'll help you, like a comrade. (*No answer*) Goodbye, then. Tell me where you end up. (*Goes.*)

(*KARL THOMAS waits for a second, all alone. FRITZ and GRETE, the children of the Landlady, open the door and look about, curiously.*)

FRITZ: May we come in?

GRETE: We'd like to look at you.

THOMAS: Sure, come on in. (*FRITZ and GRETE enter. Both regard KARL THOMAS as a strange specimen.*)

FRITZ: We've got to go soon.

GRETE: We have tickets for the cinema.

FRITZ: And for the boxing match this evening. Do you spar?

THOMAS: I don't know how to box.

FRITZ: Oh.

GRETE: Do you dance? Do you know the Charleston? The Black Bottom?

THOMAS: No, I don't know how to dance.

GRETE: That's a shame.

(*Silence*)

GRETE: Did you really spend eight years in the madhouse?

FRITZ: She wouldn't believe me when I told her.

THOMAS: Yes, I did.

GRETE: And before that, you were sentenced to death?

FRITZ: Mother told us. She read it in the paper.

THOMAS: Your mother rents these rooms?

GRETE: Of course.

THOMAS: Is your mother poor?

FRITZ: Only the racketeers are rich these days, Mother says.

THOMAS: Did she tell you why I was sentenced to death?

GRETE: Because you fought in the war.

FRITZ: No, silly goose! Because he took part in the Revolution.

THOMAS: What do you know of the war? Of the Revolution? Did your mother tell you about it?

GRETE: No. Mother never talks about it.

FRITZ: We memorized all the battles in school.

GRETE: Which day they took place. Who won.

THOMAS: Once you've fought in a war, you realize it's not about who wins and who loses. War is murder.

FRITZ: Yeah, well. We learned all about it in history class. The Thirty Years' War took place from 1618 to 1648.

GRETE: Thirty years.

FRITZ: We only had to memorize half as many battles as the World War.

GRETE: And that only lasted for four years.

FRITZ (*recites, from memory*): The Battle of Lüttich, the Battle of the Marne, the Battle of Verdun, the Battle of Tannenberg...

GRETE: Don't forget the Battle of Ypres!

THOMAS: Do you know anything else about the war?

FRITZ: That's enough.

GRETE: More than enough! I got bad marks because I mixed up 1916 and 1917.

THOMAS: And what were you taught about the Revolution?

FRITZ: We don't have as many dates there, so it's easier to memorize.

THOMAS: What does the suffering of millions mean, if the next generation is already dead to it? All information these days flows into a bottomless pit. How old are you?

GRETE: Thirteen.

FRITZ: Fifteen.

THOMAS: And your names?

FRITZ, GRETE: Fritz, Grete.

THOMAS: You know nothing about the war.

FRITZ: Oh, yes we do!

THOMAS: What building stands there, at the end of the street?

FRITZ: A factory.

THOMAS: And what do they make there?

FRITZ, GRETE:... Gas?

THOMAS: Do you know what kind of gas?

GRETE: I don't know.

FRITZ: Poison gas.

THOMAS: And what is poison gas for?

FRITZ: It's for if the enemy attacks us.

GRETE: Right, the enemy. They want to lay waste to our country.

THOMAS: And who are your enemies? (*They are silent*) Have you ever seen a person die from poison gas? They turn yellow, then they turn green, then you see them unable to breathe. When we were in the trenches, they used gas on all of us, countryman and enemies alike.

FRITZ: They didn't teach us that.

THOMAS: Give me your hand, Fritz. What would happen to this hand if a bullet pierced it?

FRITZ: That's a stupid question! It would be busted.

THOMAS: And what would happen to your face, if I sprayed a cloud of poison gas over it? Did they teach you that in school?

GRETE (*pleased to know the answer*): Yes! It would be scraped to bits. Eaten away. You'd die!

THOMAS: Would you like to die?

GRETE: You ask such funny questions. Of course not.

THOMAS: I'll tell you a story now. Not a fairy tale. A story that happened to me, in the war. I was in the trenches, some-where. And suddenly one night we heard screams, a per-son suffering from an indescribable pain. Then complete silence. It was somebody who had just died, we thought, obviously. But an hour later we heard the screams come back again, only this time they didn't stop. These screams, this man screaming, we heard him throughout the entire night. The next day, we heard this man scream-ing again, until darkness fell. It was pathetic, he was com-pletely helpless. When it got dark on the second night, two soldiers rose out of the trenches and tried to find the man who lay wounded out there, in no man's land. Suddenly, bullets rang out and both the soldiers were shot dead. Two others tried. They, too, never returned. Then orders came down that we weren't allowed to leave our trench. We had to obey. But the man, he continued to scream. We had no idea whether he was a Frenchman, a German, an Englishman—an Arab, a Kurdish man. He screamed like a baby would scream, naked, wordlessly. He screamed, it seems impossible now, for four days and four nights without stopping. It felt like four years. We stuffed paper in our ears. It didn't help. Then, the silence. I wish I could sow these images in your hearts. Can you imagine?

FRITZ: Yes.

GRETE: That poor man.

THOMAS: Yes, that poor man! Not the enemy. The man. The man screamed. In France, in Germany, in Russia, in Japan, in Iraq, in Afghanistan, in Syria, a man. At such times, when you get down to basics, you have to ask yourself: why all this war? What's it for? Wouldn't you ask the same question?

FRITZ, GRETE: Yes.

THOMAS: In every country, men have mused over the same question. In every country, men give the same answer. For oil. For land. For gas. (*Pause*) Men died for all of these dead things. They starved. They were driven to despair. That was the answer. We, as revolutionaries, stood strong, we shouted "No" to all this war. They called us cowards, they called us madmen, they called us criminals, terrorists. We fought for a world in which children could be happy and safe. But we lost. We were defeated.

(*Long pause*)

FRITZ: How many of you were there?

THOMAS: Not enough. The people didn't understand what we were fighting for. They didn't see that we were fighting for their own lives.

FRITZ: How many were there on the other side?

THOMAS: Many. And they had weapons. And money.

(*Pause*)

FRITZ: Well, you were stupid to think that you could win.

GRETE: Yes. Very stupid.

THOMAS (*stares at them*): What did you say?

FRITZ: I said you were stupid.

GRETE: Very stupid.

FRITZ: We should go now. Look alive, Grete!

GRETE: OK!

FRITZ, GRETE: Goodbye.

(*They exit. KARL THOMAS stares after them, at a total loss for words.*)

Filmic Interlude

EAST END OF A BIG CITY

FACTORIES, CHIMNEYS, QUITTING TIME

WORKERS LEAVING FACTORIES

CROWDS IN THE STREETS

Scene Two. Election Hall

WORKERS' TAVERN, AN ELECTION HALL.

The stage has been set up as a polling station. An ELECTION SUPERVISOR sits behind a table. At right, a ballot booth. At front, WORKERS sitting at tables, drinking and smoking.

WORKER 3: Look at this shit. They're swarming like flies.

WORKER 2: You're an idiot. This is democracy at work.

WORKER 3: I've voted in every election since the Kaiser abdicated. Gotten us nowhere.

WORKER 1: What else can we do? Our votes are counted, and after that we just have to hope the politicians do what they say they'll do.

WORKER 3: Only the stupidest cows elect their own butchers.

WORKER 1: What are you saying? We're just meat to the slaughter?

WORKER 2: Would both of you shut up? Or do you want a punch in the face?

ELECTION SUPERVISOR (*from back*): QUIET! My God, these people—you can't even hear yourself think! What's your name, ma'am?

OLD WOMAN: Barbara Stilzer.

SUPERVISOR: And where do you live?

OLD WOMAN: As of October first I will be living at seven, um, now, let's see, what's the name of that street…

SUPERVISOR: I need to know where you live right now.

OLD WOMAN: My landlord, I complained about him to the housing office. Ah. Right now I live at 11 Margaretenstrasse. Apartment 4A.

SUPERVISOR (*says nothing but writes down; OLD WOMAN is motionless*): You can drop off your ballot now.

OLD WOMAN: I only came because I'll be fined if I don't vote.

SUPERVISOR: Take this pencil, make a cross under the name of your candidate, and place your ballot in the box there.

OLD WOMAN: But I don't have a ballot. I didn't know I was supposed to bring one. How am I supposed to read all these words?

SUPERVISOR: Listen, I'm not the commissioner. I am just an election supervisor. The ballots are right over there. Go get one and then come back.

OLD WOMAN (*wanders downstage toward ELECTION OFFICERS.*)

ELECTION OFFICER 1: Here you go, young lady, just make your cross right under this line here. That's how you'll choose the right president. General von Landsring has promised law and order and to look after little old ladies like yourself!

OLD WOMAN (*flips the ballot over, undecided.*)

OFFICER 2: No, no, little Mother: make the cross here, under number two. Don't you want cheaper bread and gas?

OLD WOMAN: The price of gas is high. It's shocking, how much it costs to fill up your tank!

OFFICER 2: It's because of those landlords, little Mother. Vote for common sense and the people's choice. Vote number two.

OLD WOMAN (*flips the ballot over, undecided.*)

OFFICER 3: Vote number three. Law and order? Law and order is for the wealthy, not for you! Common sense? The people's choice? You can lick their hands like a dog, and they'll still sell you out to their wealthy friends as soon as they get the chance. Vote for number three, vote for the Communist Party, or you might as well tie a noose around your neck.

OLD WOMAN (*flips the ballot over, still undecided.*)

OFFICER 1: Number one!

OFFICER 2: Number two!

OFFICER 3: Number three!

(*OLD WOMAN wanders upstage.*)

SUPERVISOR: Do you have your ballot?

OLD WOMAN: Yes. I have three, actually.

SUPERVISOR: You're only allowed to have one, or your vote is invalid.

OLD WOMAN: Oh. (*Goes into the voting booth*) Can I come back out now? (*Comes out*) Good evening. (*Passes by the ELECTION OFFICERS*) All right, all right, don't get mad, I put a cross under all three!

TABLE THREE

WORKER 1: Giving women the vote. What's next? I'll tell you what a woman is good for. Three things…

WORKER 2: Back when I had steady work, things were good. I didn't used to spend all my time drinking at the bar.

WORKER 3: You still have a wife, don't you? I bet she gives it to you good, judging from the scratches on your back.

WORKER 2: She beats me, because I come home drunk and too broke to pay for food. Being on unemployment, we eat herring and marmalade four days a week.

WORKER 3: What about the other three?

WORKER 2: We hold our noses up to the wind.

WORKER 1: Ah, well. It all comes out the same. At the end of the day, it's all shit, isn't it?

THOMAS (*enters. To ELECTION SUPERVISOR*): Excuse me, is there an Albert Kroll here? I was told he works here, supervising elections.

SUPERVISOR: He was just here. He'll be back in a little bit.

KARL THOMAS: I'll wait for him. (*Sits at a table.*)

WORKER 3: I think they should all be shot and hanged, the lot of them.

WORKER 1: Yesterday I stepped outside and saw this fat lawyer and his wife standing there, you know, looking like a piece of Christmas ham, covered in grease and fat on all sides. And they looked right at me and said, "Such a pity. Those poor people."

WORKER 3: The time will come when they're the ones in need of pity.

WORKER 2: We'll show them this time, this election is the one!

AT THE VOTING TABLE

DISTINGUISHED VOTER: I won't tolerate this!

SUPERVISOR (*ruffling through papers*): I'm sorry, Mr. Secretary, there's been some mistake...

VOTER: You've cost me my vote. I will lodge an official protest! The election must be declared invalid! I will not be quieted! I will protest this to the highest levels!

SUPERVISOR: You must have been left off the voting registration through some kind of error.

VOTER: My rights must be respected! I must have my rights!

SUPERVISOR: According to the law, I'm not allowed to give you a ballot.

VOTER: Stripping me of my rights, that's what you're doing! I demand that some order be established here! I will denounce this pigsty!

SUPERVISOR: Please, Mr. Secretary, be reasonable. Think of all the unrest among the people—

VOTER: My rights are my rights.

ELECTION OFFICER 2 (*walking over*): Please, Mr. Secretary…

SUPERVISOR: As a good citizen you wouldn't want to suggest anything untoward.

VOTER: It will be in the press, in black and white. There's something else behind all this. Of course it has to happen to me, it always happens to me, always, always, always! But I have had enough!

(*KARL THOMAS, who has been listening, is about to say something when ALBERT KROLL enters, recognizing KARL THOMAS immediately.*)

ALBERT KROLL (*like he's seen a ghost*): Dear God.

THOMAS: I've found you at last.

ALBERT: Those were terrible times. For everyone.

THOMAS: You say that as if they're over.

ALBERT: Have you found work?

THOMAS: I've been to the unemployment office six times. They say I have no skills. I need to learn how to type.

I saw our old comrades, selling junk in department stores, sitting at their little posts, with their little jobs. Cashier number one—number two—number three. I tried to talk to them but they all gave me the cold shoulder. Some of them looked at me with pity and gave me money. As if all I need is money! Albert, what has become of our struggle! Department stores. You don't seem to care.

ALBERT: No. It's just that nothing surprises me now. Hold on a second, Karl. There's so much I want to ask you, but I must go upstairs. I'm on the election committee now and you wouldn't believe these officials. You can't trust those pigs not to cheat. (*Crosses to election table.*)

SUPERVISOR: New poll! The election closes in an hour and we're already at eighty percent turnout. Eighty percent!

ALBERT (*holds up a paper*): I have sworn testimony here from three hundred workers saying they were struck from the election lists.

SUPERVISOR: I can't do anything about that? Everyone living near the chemical factory had to be struck off the lists. They haven't lived there for four months.

ALBERT: That's because the chemicals were poisonous. They have a constitutional right to vote.

SUPERVISOR: The Ministry of the Interior makes the rules, not me.

ALBERT: Then I'm going to lodge an official appeal over the election.

SUPERVISOR (*on the telephone*): District Six? How many reporting? Sixty-five? We've got eighty! (*Hangs up.*) We're going straight to the top and you want to lodge a protest! Fine, see how far that gets you.

ALBERT (*goes to KARL THOMAS*): Kilman has disenfranchised hundreds of workers! And that's just the ones we were able to contact! He took the right to vote from the workers at the chemical factory!

THOMAS: How can you sit back and watch this go on?

ALBERT: We're fighting, but there aren't enough of us left. Most people have already forgotten, the rest just want peace and quiet. We need to win over hearts and minds. We need to educate, on the widest possible basis.

THOMAS: Hundred thousand unemployed...

ALBERT: Hunger creeps in one door, reason out the other. When times are hard, it's easy to find scapegoats.

THOMAS: That's not how a great leader talks.

ALBERT: Well, maybe I'm sick of great leaders. They marched us all into a mass grave, and for what? When they stopped and looked back, they realized nobody was following them anymore.

THOMAS: You sound like Kilman!

ALBERT: Kilman has something to hide. I'm telling the truth. These days, one day feels like ten. One must learn to think clearly. Are you listening to me, Karl?

THOMAS: Why should I care about the results of some stolen election! I want to see the old kind of faith, the kind that could move mountains!

ALBERT: You think I no longer have faith?

THOMAS: It's only faith that counts.

ALBERT: I'm not interested in being saved, Karl Thomas: do I need to tell you the names of all the old comrades I've seen harassed? Imprisoned? Murdered?

THOMAS: This is all wrong, all wrong. You're just a part of it now, aren't you? Just another part of the election scam.

ALBERT: I am doing what I can. No more, no less.

THOMAS: I will do what I must. I tell you, I'll make an example.

ALBERT: It takes more than one. It takes all of us. Every day of our lives.

THOMAS: That's not what I mean. One must sacrifice oneself. Only then will the weak become heroes. Countless days and nights I've spent, beating my fists against my skull. (*Darkly*) But now I know what I have to do.

ALBERT: I'm listening.

THOMAS: Come here. Quietly. (*Leans in*) Kilman's got to go.

ALBERT (*a pause as he searches Karl Thomas's face, then*): You really are useless, aren't you? (*Turns to WORKER 3*) The police confiscated our truck. They're sabotaging our attempts to get out the vote.

THOMAS (*screaming now*): Such courage! You're all cowards! All of you! I should have stayed in the madhouse!

ALBERT: I don't want to influence anybody too much. I dare not tell the whole truth.

SUPERVISOR (*to ALBERT*): You need to stop speaking to the voters. You're not allowed to influence them. (*To VOTER*) This isn't an information booth, Mr. Butcher.

ALBERT: I'm not trying to "influence" anybody. I'm just telling them the truth.

WORKER 4 (*enters*): Albert, the police have impounded our truck.

ALBERT: Why?

WORKER 4: The posters mocking the Minister of Defense.

ALBERT: Form a delegation and petition the Ministry.

WORKER 4: We did that this morning. One of our pamphleteers was arrested. Kilman isn't seeing anyone.

ALBERT: Go, go to the Ministry. Call here right away if he refuses you. (*WORKER 4 exits.*) Have you heard me, Karl? Karl? (*KARL is not listening, but rather is dazed by the carnival-like atmosphere.*)

WORKER 1: Have you voted yet?

WORKER 2: No point. Something fishy is going on there, I tell you.

WORKER 3: Needs to get worse before it can get better. Let von Landsring win. Things will get so bad that there has to be change.

SUPERVISOR (*on the phone, ignoring ALBERT*): What time do you have? Ten before nine?—Yes, yes, all smooth-sailing over here. Airtight operation. (*Hangs up.*) The fifth district is eight minutes fast. Eight minutes! Looks like we'll know the results eight minutes early.

(*WORKER 2 heads to the election table. PICKEL enters.*)

PICKEL: Excuse me, can a citizen from Holzhausen cast his vote here? (*OFFICERS surround PICKEL.*)

OFFICER 1: Law and order through the whole country, for God and our dear Fatherland! Vote for Number 1!

OFFICER 2: Wake up, sheeple, there's still time! Not the right, not the left, stand by the state! Number 2 is your man!

OFFICER 3: Our President will work for the workers and the poor! Vote for Number 3!

PICKEL: Thank you, thank you. (*Goes to the election table.*)

SUPERVISOR: What's your name?

PICKEL: Pickel.

SUPERVISOR: Where do you live?

PICKEL: In Holzhausen, which is in the municipality of Münsing.

SUPERVISOR: Your name isn't on the registry. With a B?

PICKEL: No, Pickel. With a P.

SUPERVISOR: You can't vote here. You're at the wrong polling station.

PICKEL: Yes, I live in Holzhausen, you see—

SUPERVISOR: What are you doing here, then? Next!

PICKEL (*rejected, goes to KARL THOMAS*): Excuse me, good Sir, but don't we know each other? Yes! We met in the Prime Minister's office! Prime Minister Kilman is a great man.

THOMAS: I sat next to him in prison.

PICKEL: I don't understand. What do you mean?

(*BANKER enters. BALLOT COUNTERS surround them.*)

BANKER: Thank you. (*Moves quickly through them to ELECTION SUPERVISOR.*)

SUPERVISOR: At your service, Director. Do you still live at Opernplatz?

BANKER: Yes. I'm running late, so if you don't mind, I'd like to hurry.

SUPERVISOR: There's still time, Director. Here you go, Sir. (*BANKER goes into the ballot box.*)

PICKEL: Everything is so confusing, here. In Holzhausen, we had an election, and everyone was able to vote at the local church. But here everyone is a stranger. Who knows if every vote gets counted? Who knows anything?

SUPERVISOR (*to BANKER, who has left the ballot box*): Your most devoted servant, Director. (*BANKER goes; SUPERVISOR shouts out.*) The ballot box is now closed.

WORKER 1: Gee, I wonder who will win.

WORKER 2: My money's on von Landsring to pull through. He's a war hero. He has to win.

WORKER 3: Yeah, your candidate was bribed! By foreigners! By Russians! That'll serve you all right!

WORKER 2: That's a lie! Propaganda and disinformation! Everyone knows it was the Jews!

TITLE CARD: [*scrolling update of vote totals*]

RADIO: Attention! Attention! First election result is in. Twelfth district. 714 votes for his Excellency General von Landsring, 414 votes for Minister Kilman, 67 votes for Mr. Bandke.

WORKER 2: Ouch.

WORKER 1: High-seas robbery!

WORKER 3: Bravo!

(*WORKERS 1 and 2 exit*)

PICKEL: Excuse me, Mr. Election Supervisor, Sir, but you really shouldn't shut up shop just yet. I've only just gotten here, and I am on close personal terms with Prime Minister Kilman…

SUPERVISOR: Complain to him, then. He's going to lose anyway.

PICKEL: But what if Mr. Kilman needed just one more vote? Think, if only because of my vote...

TITLE CARD: [scrolling update of vote totals]

RADIO: Attention! Attention! Message from Osthafen. Six thousand for Bandke. Four thousand for Minister Kilman, two thousand for his Excellency von Landsring.

MOB ON THE STREET (shouts from offstage): Hooray! Hooray!

THOMAS: What are they cheering about? How can anyone take joy in counting votes? What kind of accomplishment is that? Nothing will change, if anything, things will only get worse.

ALBERT: Accomplishment—no. But you need to take a first step somewhere.

THOMAS: You disgust me.

TITLE CARD: Attention! Attention!

RADIO: Attention! Attention! From the capital: the latest results hand Minister Kilman the majority.

MOB: Hooray for Kilman! Hooray for Kilman!

WORKER 2: Didn't I tell you? You're buying the next round!

WORKER 1: We only talked about coming here for one drink.

WORKER 2: Cheap ass!

PICKEL: Excuse me, but I still haven't cast my vote... Mr. Prime Minister, if he had my vote... this election...

OFFICER 1: Gentlemen, we've beaten the record. Ninety-seven percent turnout! Ninety-seven percent!

THOMAS: If only I understood! Is everyone insane?

RADIO: Attention! Attention! We will announce the result at nine-thirty.

WORKER 2: I bet it's Kilman. Who's with me?

PICKEL: If only I had a vote...

OFFICER 1: We've got to get this in the newspaper! Ninety-seven percent! That has never happened before! It's miraculous!

PICKEL: If I could have voted...

(*Tumult outside. WORKERS enter.*)

WORKER 4: They've killed Mother Meller!

WORKER 5: The fiends!

ALBERT: What's going on?

WORKER 5: She was protesting with the workers outside and tried to nail a pamphlet on the wall of the factory.

WORKER 4: The police hit her with a truncheon! An old woman.

WORKER 3: Dropped her right there on the sidewalk, she was out!

WORKER 5: Since when has it been a crime to post pamphlets?

WORKER 3: Good question! When will we have a free election!

WORKER 4: Bang, right on the head. An old woman.

THOMAS: Do you hear that?

ALBERT: Make way, comrades.

(*ALBERT KROLL moves toward the door. The WORKERS bring an unconscious MOTHER MELLER. ALBERT lays her on the ground.*)

ALBERT: A pillow... water!... She fainted. She's alive.

WORKER 4: Not a word of warning. With a truncheon. An old woman.

ALBERT: Coffee!

WORKER 5: What about the constitution! They'll answer for this.

WORKER 3: To whom? You're naïve, man.

ALBERT: Mother Meller! Easy now. This is Karl Thomas. Do you remember him?

MOTHER MELLER: Karl... You look exactly the same.

ALBERT: What happened?

MELLER: One of the pamphlets—the "i" hadn't been dotted. Then this man with a truncheon—(*Waking up, suddenly realizing*) They've arrested Eva! (*More tumult outside.*)

(*WORKERS 1 and 3 enter with RAND.*)

WORKER 1: Here he is! We got the dirty rat!

WORKER 3: I know him. He's a regular at our meetings. The most radical.

WORKER 1: A spy!

MORE WORKERS (*attacking RAND*): Get him! Get him!

ALBERT (*grabs RAND by the arm*): Quiet!

THOMAS: Here's your election victory, right here! (*KARL moves to strike RAND. ALBERT holds KARL off.*)

ALBERT: Karl, wait!

WORKER 5: No, let's kill him!

ALBERT: What are we? A pack of wild dogs?

RAND: Thank you, Mr. Kroll.

ALBERT: Your face—I know you.

RAND: I was your warden once, a long time ago.

MELLER: Oh my God. What a happy reunion! We ought to have a cup of coffee and catch up.

RAND: I treated you kindly, didn't I? You must admit that.

ALBERT: Yes, I remember you. "I'm only following orders; it'll all be over soon."

(*WORKERS laugh*)

RAND: What was I supposed to do? I'm a working man, just like you. I have a wife. Children. A salary that makes me sick. I was just following orders.

ALBERT: And whose orders are you following now?

RAND: Direct orders from Minister Kilman.

WORKER 1: Here's the revolver we got off him.

(*KARL THOMAS grabs the revolver and turns it on RAND as if he's about to shoot him. ALBERT KROLL slaps his arm.*)

ALBERT: Stop this insanity! (*MOTHER MELLER holds KARL THOMAS close.*) What's inside your jacket? (*Pulls a bundle of pamphlets from RAND'S waistcoat, reads*): "Comrades, beware the Jews!"—"Alien Enemy Elements!"—"Shun the Elders of Zion!"—Good to see you've got your beliefs.

RAND: It is the Jews—

ALBERT: Come on! Up! Get out of here! I've saved you once, I can't be expected to do so a second time—even if I wanted to. (*RAND exits.*)

THOMAS: Mother Meller, let go of me! I just want to talk... Albert, why did you stop them?

ALBERT: There is strength in patience.

THOMAS: You're a coward, all of you—cowards! Why bother being alive? All for a bunch of cowardly vote-stealers?

ALBERT: You are a fool. The world isn't always a fireworks show, Karl, with rockets and flares going off.

THOMAS: You disgust me.

ALBERT: You're the one who refuses to see the world as it is. You need to find some work, Karl. Mother Meller, take him in.

MELLER: Don't you have a place to stay? The hotel where I work needs a bus-boy. I'll speak to the head-waiter.

ALBERT: Take her advice, Karl. You need to make a go of everyday life.

MELLER: I miss you.

ALBERT: We can share a cup of coffee any day.

TITLE CARD: Attention! Attention!

(*The RADIO fails. Buzzing noises*)

PICKEL: I just want to go back to Holzhausen.

RADIO: The Secretary of State, General von Landsring, was elected by a large majority to be President of the Republic.

Screams and songs in the street.
A portrait of the President appears on the horizon.

Intermission

ACT THREE

Scene One. Count and Student

A SMALL ROOM. *STUDENT reading. Someone knocks.*

STUDENT: Who's there? Count Lande!

LANDE (*enters*): Pop quiz: what do you think of our new president, von Landsring?

STUDENT: He's one of us. He has our best intentions at heart.

COUNT: But he's no good to us so long as Kilman remains in power at the Ministry. He'll have no power to change things.

STUDENT: Can that be true?

COUNT: Do you have a cigarette? (*Pauses as the STUDENT lights him a cigarette.*) I've been thinking. (*Exhales.*) We should dissolve our little "group."

STUDENT: What? How can you say that!

COUNT: Kilman.

STUDENT: Something must be done. We always talk about doing the "great deed," but, now, when we're so close.

COUNT: Hush. (*Holds a hand up to his lips, crosses to the window.*) Can anyone else hear us in here?

STUDENT: No. What is it?

COUNT: Here. (*Gives STUDENT a paper.*)

STUDENT: Orders?

COUNT: Read. (*Pause*) You must be ready to strike at any moment.

STUDENT: So. It's come to this. So fast.

COUNT: You hesitate? Isn't this what you always wanted? Isn't this the life you chose? Don't you want to stop the enemies of our freedom? How quickly they forget! This was the same Kilman who was lined up against the wall eight years ago on charges of high treason against the Fatherland—and today he's sitting in power at the Reichstag. How is it that a man can lose an election and still maintain power over his shadowy cabal? It's this damn parliamentary system we have. And you hesitate to act!

STUDENT: No. I'm not hesitating. It's just that—it doesn't feel right, having to wait. The deed should be done now.

COUNT: You need to learn how to curb your lust.

STUDENT: But what if I'm arrested?

COUNT: We can help you make it to the border. And if you don't make it, you must be prepared. To sacrifice yourself. We have your best interests at heart, my young friend. Never doubt that you have truth and justice on your side.

STUDENT: Can I leave a letter for my mother?

COUNT: Impossible. The cause must not be undermined by any stray remarks. One must be vigilant against cowards, for compromisers in our midst. They would rat us out in a second if they smelled the opportunity.

STUDENT: I don't understand politics. I became a soldier as soon as I came of age, and a month later it all came crashing down. I hated the revolution, just as I hate this democracy. My uncle was a general. I worshipped him like a god. Three days after the revolution this dog came in to speak to us. "I'm from the Soldiers' Councils," he said. "Your golden epaulets are provoking the people in the streets. From this day forward, there will be no more epaulets. All of our shoulders will stand naked." My uncle stood up, took out his sword, and laid it on the table. I could see the old man trembling. His eyes were moist. The very next day, my uncle shot himself. He had nothing left to live for. And that soldier, the smug little rat from the Soldiers' Council, was none other than Wilhelm Kilman!

COUNT: The scoundrel!

STUDENT: He left behind a suicide note: "I cannot live to see the shame of our Fatherland. May my death open the eyes of the brainwashed people."

COUNT: We have all been disgraced, just like your uncle. And the people have been brainwashed, helping traitors, such as this Kilman, rise to power... I promise, you will have vengeance.

(*Blackout*)

Scene Two. The Hotel

FAÇADE OF THE GRAND HOTEL.

The wall opens, allowing us to see all the rooms simultaneously. In the main ballroom, dancing couples, the sound of a jazz band.

The main theme of the show plays:

[F*#@ It, We're Alive!]
(lyrics by Walter Mehring, music by Edmund Meisel)

In the finest Hotel on the Planet
Where the crème de la crème are the guests—
Where everything is light and easy
And there's no thought of troublesome pests—
Fine food and drink, no expenses are spared—
Until the war is declared
And the checks they start to bounce!

Here come the diplomatic attachés
To debate the fine affairs of the state,
They say: we really need to end this peace,
The time is now, send out the press release!

And when asked, they describe their policy:
Fuck it, we're alive!—
We're alive and we've done the math:

Sabre-rattling—populism—
What's the dance you'll dance tomorrow?
Fuck it!

Poison gases—genocide—
Apocalyptic fratricide!
Fuck it!

Our hearts begin to bleed and stink
From all the printer's useless ink,
Fuck it!

We're free now—shackled in our worker's quarters —
We should have stayed and been blown up by mortars!
Fuck it! We're alive!

In the finest Hotel on the Earth
Where Generals are given the loftiest perch—
We try to tell them, look what you've done to us!
They tell us, don't make such a fuss!
They see our bleeding stumps,
They tip us, we're a garbage dump,
More fit to fill up a mass grave—

And when asked who's best to pay the bill,
For all this agony and overkill,
Here comes the Secretary of Defense,
And the church to preach some common sense,
They lead us in song, the holy choir sings:
Fuck it! We're alive!—
We're alive, and we've done the math!

The Generals blame the Communists,
We'll make them cease and desist.
Fuck it!

And the millions who've been murdered—
All our fears and worries,
Fuck it!

Our hearts they turn to ice,
Crushed by the iron vice,
Fuck it!
Freedom—under capitalism—
Suicide! Paroxysm!
Fuck it! We're alive!

In the finest Hotel on the Planet
Where the crème de la crème are the guests—
Where everything is light and easy
And there's no thought of troublesome pests—
The enemies are taken out and beaten—
And the homeless are given scraps to eat-en!
We take seriously our charitable deeds!

The ministers, the thinkers, and the speakers:
They're all the same faces, they've got us hook and sinker!
It's all the same, like it was just before the war—
Right in time for World War Two!
Fascism! Marching in the streets!
Listen up, comrades!
It's no time for us to make a retreat!

If we destroy this world of sorrow,
What's the dance you'll see tomorrow?
Fuck it!

If it's us instead of them,
What say you then,
Fuck it!

Seek protection from your gods,
Electrified world falls apart,
Fuck it!

Away with all these leaders,
New commands:
Fuck it! We're alive!
And we've done the math!

[*Alternate final verse*]
In the finest hotel in the world
Where murder and war are all around,
There huddled in the basement floor,
The workers are all doing their chores,
They need to pay their bills
With blood and guts and their last wills,
Starving, freezing,
And dying—
Fuck it!

SERVANTS' ROOM

(*KARL THOMAS sits at table in a waiter's uniform. MOTHER MELLER enters.*)

MELLER: Here, Karl, I brought you some soup. It was sent back from someone's room. I reheated it.

THOMAS: Thank you. I only have a five-minute break.

MELLER (*stops in the doorway*): Oh, Karl, you look so different in that outfit, ten years younger almost, like a ghost. I didn't recognize you at first.

THOMAS (*laughs*).

MELLER (*frightened*): But why are you laughing?

THOMAS: Don't worry. I'm not crazy again. Everywhere I've been to look for work, they always ask me, "Why such a look of death, man? It scares the customers! In times like these one must always be smiling! Always be laughing!" So, I went to see a stylist. And voila: my new façade! Don't I look good enough to eat?

MELLER: I'll admit, at first I found it uncanny. Who knows? Maybe they'll make us sign contracts, so we have to be laughing for ten hours straight. Anyways, I must get back.

PRIVATE ROOM. BANKER, BANKER'S SON, HEAD-WAITER, PAGE.

HEAD-WAITER: Your menu, Sir. Anything special tonight, Director?

BANKER: Something light. Nothing too heavy, my stomach—maybe a little chicken broth.

HEAD-WAITER: As you wish. (*Exits*)

SON: I still have doubts.

BANKER: How are you going to make your way in the world without a wife? And Lotte is very pretty. What is there to lose?

SON: She's too—complicated. Last night, she was telling stories of working as a kitchen cook at government banquets!

BANKER: Who cares what she used to do? Nowadays, money is the only thing. It doesn't matter what her father used to be—what matters is who her father is now. Besides, if you marry her, I'll get cheap credit from the state as long as he's in office.

SON: So you think.

BANKER: My dear boy, you don't have an audience with a Minister every day. They don't give out titles and medals. Nowadays, the only foundation is money.

(*Enter KILMAN and WIFE, accompanied by HEAD-WAITER and KARL THOMAS, wearing waiter's uniform, who helps take off their outer garments.*)

BANKER: Good evening, Minister. Always delightful to see you.

KILMAN (*brusquely*): Sorry for being late. Work, as usual. People always imagine me sitting in a lounge chair and smoking fat cigars. They never see the job for what it is.

(*ALL sit. HEAD-WAITER brings food; KARL THOMAS helps.*)

MRS. KILMAN: What is this?

BANKER: A petit rien, Madame. I've taken the liberty of bringing you a rose.

MRS. KILMAN: A rose made of gold and set with pearls!

BANKER: A golden rose. My favorite kind.

MRS. KILMAN: Really, Director, this is too kind, but I can't accept.

KILMAN: You really shouldn't have.

BANKER: No need to make a fuss. Yesterday I happened to be at an auction and bought three of these. 18th century. Louis Quatorze. I already have two or three myself.

MRS. KILMAN: They are very nice. But please take them back.

KILMAN: You know those wagging tongues! We must avoid even the appearance of impropriety.

BANKER: I'm sorry, I didn't mean to—

KILMAN (*takes the rose from MRS. KILMAN's hand*): A toast! We can admire the gold rose when we come to visit you in your office.

BANKER: To your health, Madame. And yours, Minister.—Waiter, bring us some more champagne, your most expensive Mouton Rothschild. (*Blackout*)

[*CLUB ROOM. This scene was cut from the 1927 production*]

A group of PSYCHOLOGISTS and INTELLECTUALS, debating.

PHILOSOPHER X: I conclude: where quality is lacking, quantity does not provide the answer. Birth rate is not the question, but the quality of those who are born. My recommendation: nobody should marry below their social or ethnic station. What are we experiencing now, gentlemen? Nothing other than negative succession, the replacement and debasement of the genetic stock. The bare necessity for every marriage should be equality of birth, according to one's proper social caste. We have placed our trust in instinct, but sadly, instinct has proven itself to be one-sided. It will not be easy, perhaps it will take two hundred years, but we can breed a new and improved generation.

POET Y: Where did you find that in Marx?

PHILOSOPHER X: The instincts of man must be refined and spiritualized, they must have more vital spirits, more brute force, they must strive evermore toward excellence, toward the master race.

POET Y: I repeat: where did you find that in Marx?

PHILOSOPHER X: Only thus will the poor, sunken white race be helped back on its feet again. Only thus can the finer Teutonic spirits blossom as they did, once. Some will ask, how can we recognize one who has purer blood than another? But I say, he who is unable to judge the blood purity of himself or others is beyond all help. They have become lacking in the finer instincts. I personally believe they should be euthanized. That is the great thing about my Academy of Wisdom: some, it makes wise. Others, who frolic from knowledge to ignorance, it leads to their own voluntary extinction. If my recommendations are taken as necessary precautions, Good shall overcome evil, once and for all.

CALLS: Bravo! Bravo! Point of order!

PRESIDENT: Poet Y has the floor.

POET Y: Gentlemen! As we are gathered here together as equals in intellect and spirit, I ask whether our the provocation of Philosopher X helps our essential task in any way: namely, the spiritual redemption of the proletariat. As Marx has written—

CRITIC Z: There you go again, always spouting off about Marx!

POET Y: Mr. President, may I have the liberty to speak? Yes, I have read Marx, and I've found that he's no fool. Certainly, he lacked the sensibility for the new objectivity—

CLUB PRESIDENT: You are not addressing the meeting's agenda. You do not have the floor.

POET Y: Then I shall go. And all of you can kiss my ass! (*Goes*)

CALLS: Outrageous! Outrageous!

PHILOSOPHER X: Fine words from a poet!

CRITIC Z: He should go into psychoanalysis. After all, poetry is nothing more than the repression of various complexes.

PICKEL (*enters*): Well now, hello—say, am I in the right place?

PRESIDENT: No, you are not. This is a closed society.

PICKEL: Closed?—But I thought this hotel was open for business—wait a second—

CALLS: Leave us alone!

PICKEL: Thank you kindly, my good Sirs. (*Exits*)

PRESIDENT: What do you propose, Philosopher X?

PHILOSOPHER X: A short postscript, gentlemen. I will leave you with an example, to prove my point. My friend, the Poet, questioned the relationship between my remarks and the task that we have set ourselves, the spiritual redemption of the proletariat. These days, unbroken, primitive instincts can only be found among the lower depths of the social classes. We should ask a real proletarian, such as a waiter, and then I shall rest, my theory having been proven.

CALLS: Waiter! Waiter!

THOMAS (*appears with a tray, carrying glasses and bottles*): What is it? The head-waiter will be coming soon.

CALLS: You must stay.

THOMAS: I have rooms waiting for me, gentlemen.

PHILOSOPHER X: Listen to me, comrade. You are a young proletarian, aren't you?

THOMAS: Well, I—

PHILOSOPHER X: We have a question for you. Would you be willing to have coitus, sexual intercourse, with the first woman you met, or would you first consult with your instincts?

THOMAS (*laughs*).

PRESIDENT: There's no need to laugh. The question is a serious one. Also, we are your guests and you are our waiter.

THOMAS: Ah, first it was "comrade" and now I need to know my place. So you seek to redeem the proletariat? Here in the Grand Hotel? Let me ask you, then: Where were you when it started? Where would you be if it were to happen again? Right back here, in the Grand Hotel! You are eunuchs, all of you!

CALLS: Outrageous! Outrageous! (*KARL THOMAS goes.*)

PHILOSOPHER X: Petty bourgeois ideologue!

PRESIDENT: In any event, we must move on to the second item of our agenda. The proletarian community of love and the role of the intellectual. (*Blackout*)

TELEGRAPH OFFICE

TELEGRAPH OPERATOR: At last you've come! I rang three times.

THOMAS: Busy night.

OPERATOR: Telegram for Minister Kilman. It's urgent.

THOMAS: Can you hear the entire world from up here? Who are you listening to now?

LOUDSPEAKER (*a voice, like the screech of a bird of prey*): Royal Shell 104, Standard Oil 102, Rand Mines 116. Alaska Mississippi (*Image of the New York Stock Exchange*)

THOMAS: What in the world is that?

OPERATOR: The New York Stock Exchange. — They're calling out the latest prices of gas. I'll change the channel. Latest news messages from all around the world

LOUDSPEAKER (*sound of Sirens and alarms, muffled cheers: "Hoppla!"*): Attention! Attention! Uproar in India... turmoil in China... revolt in Africa... Paris! Paris! Houbigant, the stylish perfume... Bucharest! Bucharest! Famine in Romania... Berlin! Berlin! The elegant ladies delight in green wigs... New York! New York! The greatest bombing plane invented in the world. Capable of turning the capitals of Europe into rubble in seconds... Attention! Attention! Paris! London! Rome! Berlin! Calcutta! Tokyo! New York! Gentlemen drink Mumm Extra Dry...

PICTURE: (*an armored American warship*)

THOMAS: A warship—enough, enough! Please, switch it off!

OPERATOR: I'll change the channel.

LOUDSPEAKER: Brot, Brot! (*In Russian: "Bread, bread!"*)

PICTURE: (starving women and children crowded around an administrative building in Albania.)

THOMAS: Where is that?

OPERATOR: Romania, I think.

THOMAS: But they're—they're starving!

OPERATOR: People are starving to death all over the world.

THOMAS: What! As we're speaking? (*Hands in his face.*) That can't be true. You have to do something!

OPERATOR: Like what?—Just be happy that you have something to eat. (*Changes the channel.*) Where have you been the last few years, anyway?

LOUDSPEAKER (*a jumble of confused cries*): Hey, hey, hey! feste, feste, feste!... they're drowning! they're drowning!... Robbery! (*A bell*) He's pulling ahead! He's pulling ahead... MacNamara! Tonani! MacNamara!...Eviva, Eviva!...

OPERATOR: Six days in Milan... A win for MacNamara, Tonanl ...

THOMAS: I was—in a small village.

LOUDSPEAKER (*Chinese words, very quickly, with the sound of laughter*)

PICTURE: (*Chinese rebels being dragged to execution*)

THOMAS: Stop it! Turn it off!—I can't bear it!—

OPERATOR: We are helpless, don't you see? There's too much chaos in the world for any one person to make a difference.

LOUDSPEAKER (*the sound of death cries.*)

PICTURE: (*the executioner strikes*)

THOMAS: I can't stand it anymore. Turn it off! Switch it off!

OPERATOR: Civilization marches on. I'll change the channel. Play something uplifting. Roman. Midnight fare.

LOUDSPEAKER (*plays the bells of Peterskirche, sacred music, choirs.*)

PICTURE: (*a priest in white robes, above a kneeling crowd. Behind, two altar boys.*)

LOUDSPEAKER (*Latin sayings, the bells of Mass, then a few words in Latin.*)

OPERATOR: Telegraphists are sitting by all over the world, listening to the ticking of code in their headphones. Oh—this is sort of interesting. The first commercial plane from New York to Paris just radioed. A passenger is suffering from a heart attack. He's requesting a heart specialist. And you can hear his heartbeat on the radio.

FILM: The Machine-Man.

LOUDSPEAKER: (*sound of a beating heart.*)

PICTURE: *The airplane over the ocean. A beating heart.*

THOMAS: A man's heartbeat, in the middle of the ocean—

OPERATOR: It's a beautiful thing.

THOMAS: It's incredible! And what does humanity do with all of this technology? All of these possibilities?—We live like sheep, a thousand years behind!

OPERATOR: We'll never change. Did you know, I devised a method for making gasoline out of coal. I bought a patent, and what did they do? Our magnates of industry? Use it for great innovations? No. They destroyed it!—You need to go now. The telegram for the Minister is urgent. Who knows what tomorrow will bring? Maybe a war.

THOMAS: War?

OPERATOR: These things only help people kill themselves, you know. The discovery of electricity, and what did it lead to? The electric chair. There are machines running right now on electric current in London that could reduce all of Berlin into rubble tomorrow. No. Mankind will never change. Now come on, hurry up.

THOMAS: Yes, yes.

PRIVATE ROOM

BANKER: Where have you been hiding yourself with the champagne?

THOMAS: Forgive me, Sir, I was delayed. (*Hands telegram to KILMAN.*)

BANKER: Do you smoke, Madame?

MRS. KILMAN: No, thank you.

KILMAN: This brings it to a head. They've refused us concessions on gasoline!

BANKER: I sniffed it out yesterday and told my clients to sell off their Turkish shares.—How do you invest your money, Mr. Minister?

KILMAN (*laughs at him*): In bonds. I don't speculate.

BANKER: Speculation? You're the Minister of the Interior, Sir! You need to project a certain figure.

KILMAN: As a civil servant—

BANKER: We're all private individuals, aren't we? What has the state ever given back to you? Why don't you take advantage of your knowledge? It didn't stop men such as Bismarck, Disraeli—

KILMAN: I don't—

BANKER: I'll give you an example. The Ministry of Finance decides to cut funding on futures. You sell your shares at the right moment. Who could blame you if you were to sell some more? It doesn't even have to be done under your name.

KILMAN: You need to stop with this kind of talk—

BANKER: It would be my honor to advise you. You can trust me.

KILMAN (*not recognizing KARL THOMAS*): Excuse me, waiter, where is the press conference being held?

THOMAS: In the press room.

KILMAN: Tell Baron Friedrich I'd like to speak to him before he speaks to the press. (*Exits with KARL THOMAS to CORRIDOR.*)

PICKEL (*in the CORRIDOR, seeing KILMAN*): Oh, Mr. Minister! I'm so happy to see you!

KILMAN: I don't have time for this. (*Shoving past him.*)

PICKEL: Well now, really, you should be thanking me. I would have voted for you if I could! (*Exits*)

PRESS ROOM

KARL THOMAS in the doorway.

BARON FRIEDRICH: Gentlemen of the press, what was once the task of historians is now yours: to present our country's actions as the only way out, as a moral necessity. In this difficult time for our Fatherland, every newspaper must perform its duty. We do not seek war. Let me emphasize that again. We do not seek war. But these so-called sanctions which have been levied against us test our patience. When the integrity and prestige of our state is called into question—and let me repeat: we do not seek war—but when the integrity of our state is called into question, we will be forced to act.

ROOM #69

LOTTE and COUNT LANDE are lying in bed, post-coital.

COUNT: I saw you. Clear as day. Ogling the blonde at the next table.

LOTTE: Are you threatened by her? Afraid I'll betray you with her?

COUNT: Don't say such things. It disgusts me.

LOTTE: Maybe it's you men who disgust me. Maybe you've started to bore me.

COUNT: But Lotte, darling—

LOTTE: Only women know how to please another in bed. I don't deny it. I'd like to have her. She's like a little doll.

COUNT: You're drunk.

LOTTE: I would be if you weren't so cheap.

COUNT: Well, then. Let's have them bring up another bottle.

LOTTE: Please, don't. I'd prefer that little blonde – or some cocaine.

COUNT: Get dressed. I'll ring the Waiter.

(KARL THOMAS enters).

COUNT: What took you so long? A bottle of champagne, chilled.

WAITERS' BREAK ROOM

(*Sitting at supper: HEAD-WAITER, KARL THOMAS, PORTER, PAGE*)

HEAD-WAITER: At the races in Paris first place went to Mussolini. Thoroughbred. Three years old.

PORTER: Two hundred for the winner; eighty-four to place.

WAITER (*shouting from offstage*): Three more rib-eyes!

HEAD-WAITER (*shouting to the kitchen*): Three ribeyes!—Did you have money on it?

PORTER: Of course. You can't get fat from the scraps they give you here.

WAITER 2 (*shouting from off*): Six more oxtail soups! Champagne, make it a double!

HEAD-WAITER (*shouting*): Six more oxtail! And a double champagne!

THOMAS (*Puts down his spoon in disgust*): What do they put in this soup?

PORTER: I suppose you'd rather eat filet mignon?

WAITER 3 (*shouting from off*): Two dozen oysters!

HEAD-WAITER (*shouting*): Two dozen oysters!

THOMAS: I'm not demanding oysters, but this food—why doesn't the union do something?

PORTER: They're working arm in arm with the management. It's all the same to me. I make demands on nobody. Live my life like a freeman. Every day like it's my last. Before this recession, this inflation, I used to save a gold mark every week. Whenever I had ten dollars, I went to the bank and asked them to give me one gold piece. On Sunday, I'd polish it, and on Monday I'd put it in the savings bank. 600 weeks, I saved! For twelve years! And what did I end up with? Jack shit! 700 million on paper, and I couldn't buy a box of matches. People like us, the ones at the bottom, always end up getting dragged through the muck.

HEAD-WAITER: I bet they're drinking good stuff in the Private Room.

THOMAS (*sticking his hand in a pocket, fingering his gun.*)

KILMAN: "The People's Minister."

HEAD-WAITER: He must have a reason good for drinking with the banker, or he wouldn't be the Minister.

PAGE (*enters*): That man in Room 101! Always grabbing my ass.

HEAD-WAITER: Don't mind him. You know where you earn your money. (*Bell rings*) Karl, go up and see what that is.

CORRIDOR

PICKEL (*standing on the stairs.*) I can't even afford a room here, and the Prime Minister won't talk to me! You know, I thought I would like it here in the big city. I thought they would take time to hear the opinions of an ordinary citizen. (*He sees KARL THOMAS passing by.*) Hey, waiter, waiter!

THOMAS: Sorry, no time...

PICKEL: No time, no time...

SERVANTS' ROOM

(*KARL THOMAS sits alone at the table, head in his hands. MOTHER MELLER opens the door softly.*)

MELLER: Tired? (*KARL THOMAS doesn't move*) I know. It's exhausting, the first day.

THOMAS (*jumps up, rips the tie from his neck, pulls off his tailcoat and throws it in a corner, laughing as he does so*): There!—And there!—And there!

MELLER: What are you doing? You need to calm down, Karl.

THOMAS: Calm down? I've only just realized that I'm awake, and that I'll never fall asleep! I can see now how stupid I've been, just like Albert Kroll was saying. I tried to be patient, but in just half a day I've seen it all, splayed out in evening dress and nightgowns. You're all asleep! You all need something to wake you up! If this is what thinking clearly looks like, then I should go back to the madhouse! You all need something that can wake you up! All of you! (*Bell rings. A pause.*)

MELLER: Karl—

THOMAS: I won't answer that damn bell one more time! Let them all go to hell!

(*Bell rings again*).

MELLER: It's the private room. Kilman.

THOMAS: Private room? Kilman?—Then I'll go. (*Dresses himself hastily.*)

MELLER: Karl, I have to go, but I'll be back soon. We must talk about all of this. (*Exits.*)

THOMAS (*alone, pulls out and regards his revolver*): Oh, yes. I have something that will wake them all up!

(*Blackout*)

HALF-DARK CORRIDOR

STUDENT (*looking around nervously*).

COUNT (*comes out of his room*): He's in the private room. You have the waiter's uniform?

STUDENT (*opens his coat*): Yes.

COUNT: Now remember, it has to be quick. You must not be arrested. If you have bad luck, then you—you can't give any statements, understand me?

STUDENT (*nods*).

COUNT: You'll have to silence yourself.

STUDENT: I've given my word of honor.

(*Blackout*)

PRIVATE ROOM

KILMAN (*laughing at a joke*): Hahahahaha—look at my wife. How red she is! She doesn't understand... hahahahahaha.

(*Enter KARL THOMAS*).

BANKER: Finally, waiter! Another bottle of cognac, please... Why are you standing there? Well, what are you looking at? Didn't you hear me?

THOMAS: Don't you recognize me?

KILMAN: Who are you?

THOMAS: We once stood together, above a mass grave, and now, you are ashamed to say you know me?

KILMAN: Oh, it's you—don't say such stupid things, Karl. You sound like a crazy person. Come to see me tomorrow at the Ministry.

THOMAS: No. You will speak to me tonight.

KILMAN (*to BANKER*): It's alright. He's just a dreamer, someone I used to know. He showed up today, talking as if it were still 1919. He got thrown off-track by a romantic episode from our youth. He doesn't have a firm grip on reality anymore.

THOMAS: I'm waiting.

KILMAN: What is it that you can't understand? Must I tell you once more that times have changed?

BANKER: Should I send for the Hotel Manager?

KILMAN: For God's sake, no, we don't want to cause a scene. Listen, Karl, the world doesn't behave according to some utopian manifesto. You curse the way the world is, but you've never really asked yourself whether it's your own ideas that are the false ones.

BANKER: Are you in a bad way, friend? Here, take some money.

KILMAN: I'll chip in, too.

THOMAS: Money! All anyone does is just give me money! As if that will save the world! (*Holding the revolver in his pocket, looks, stunned at the offer of money, twitches his shoulders in disgust, as if he no longer wants to do the deed he wanted to commit and, tired, is turning away.*) It isn't worth it. This whole thing is meaningless.

(*The door opens. STUDENT enters in Waiter's uniform. Raises his revolver over KARL THOMAS' shoulder. Switches off the light. Shot. Screams.*)

ACT FOUR

Scene One. Outside the Hotel

OUTSIDE OF THE HOTEL. A PARK.

KARL THOMAS running after the STUDENT.

THOMAS: Hey! You! (*STUDENT turns his head, continues running*) Stop! I can help you, comrade!

STUDENT: Comrade? I am not your comrade.

THOMAS: But—but you shot at Kilman—

STUDENT: Because he's a Bolshevik. A revolutionary. He's selling our country to the Jews.

THOMAS (*takes a stunned step toward him*): Has the world become a madhouse? The world has become a madhouse!!!

STUDENT: Stay back, or I'll shoot you too!

(*STUDENT runs away, jumps into a car, leaving THOMAS struggling to comprehend. In a sudden flash, he pulls the revolver out of his pocket and shoots twice after the car. Then, recovering, he sits, forlorn, in front of a tree.*)

THOMAS: Are you a beech tree? Or are you a rubber wall? (*Touches it.*) You feel like a beech tree, rough, cracked bark, and I can smell the earth on you. But tell me: are you really a beech tree?... They shoot at him because he's a Bolshevik, a revolutionary, a Jew—and I, I shoot at the murderer of the same man that I wanted to murder myself...

(*Sits on a bank*) My head. Pounding like cannon-fire. The carousel spins around and around—a bullet in the head, spinning around and around.—The bell rings and the ride begins again. Around we go, one shot, two shots. Shoot out the lights! I am lost to the world, and the world is lost to me. (*Holds revolver to his temple*) Stop, stop! (*Throws revolver down in disgust; sound of a fire alarm, emergency responders trying to save KILMAN's life*) If the house is on fire, let's sit back and watch the bucket brigade douse the flames with gasoline. We can watch them rise higher and higher— (*Fire alarm*) Ring the alarm!—All over the city!—Stir up the crowds—wake the dead!—They're all asleep, lying on their bellies like pigs, snoring into their pillows—some see shadows in the night, but I see killers, bare brains spilled out on the floor, starving hysterical naked—oh, why did they let me out of that madhouse? Why open the door and shove me inside? It was so nice inside there, despite the cold, despite this beating of wings inside my head—it never stops.

(*Puts gun to his head again*) I have lost my grip on the world. And the world—has lost—its grip—on me— (*about to pull the trigger.*)

(*During the last sentence TWO POLICEMEN enter and grab him*)

POLICEMAN 1: Hey, what are you doing over there? Don't you know you're not supposed to walk on the grass?

POLICEMAN 2: Hold on. (*Whispers in the ear of the other policeman.*) What's that? I suppose you just happened upon this gun?

THOMAS: What do I know? What do you know? A gun turns against its owner, and nothing comes out but the sound of laughter.

POLICEMAN 2: Talk some sense. Do you understand me?

THOMAS: Oh, yes. You see, I once thought that if I walked straight through the park I could get to the hotel. Order a cup of coffee. Two dollars and fifty cents. I thought I was going somewhere? But you know where I ended up? In a madhouse.

POLICEMAN 1: You're under arrest.

THOMAS: Let go of me!

POLICEMAN 2: There's no sense resisting.

POLICEMAN 1: Don't try to escape.

POLICEMAN 2: Did you shoot the minister?

THOMAS: Me?

POLICEMAN 1: Yes, you.

POLICEMAN 2: Let's take him to the station.

(*Blackout. Sounds of the cries of a mob*)

Scene Two. Police Office

POLICE COMMISSIONER'S OFFICE. *Telephone rings.*

COUNT (*on telephone*): Count Lande here, my dear Commissioner. I'm so glad I was able to reach you in person.

COMMISSIONER: By all means, Count! At your disposal.

COUNT: I just wanted to verify the news reports... the Minister's been killed and the attacker arrested. Right?

COMMISSIONER: Yes.

COUNT: And they say he is a nationalist—um, a right-wing—student—?

COMMISSIONER: Ooooooh? Oh no, it was certainly a leftist of some kind.

COUNT: Ah, but—I thought—

COMMISSIONER: Of course, that's just my personal intuition.

COUNT: Ah, okay then—good. Good! I mean, that's terrible, obviously. And they say—he was wearing a waiter's uniform?

COMMISSIONER: Do they? (*Grabs a notebook.*)

COUNT: Yes. But you didn't hear it from me.

COMMISSIONER: May I ask where I can reach you, if I need more information?

COUNT: Grand Hotel. Room 69.

COMMISSIONER (*hangs up. Telephones*): You stay. All stations keep watch for any armed protests—from the left, of course!

ASSISTANT (*enters*): Commissioner, we found a man behaving very strangely. He was arrested in a corridor of the Grand Hotel, although he isn't listed as staying there as a guest. He was seen with Minister Kilman just before the attack. He cannot say why, precisely, it's hard to understand him.—If you can believe it, he demands you come see him.

COMMISSIONER: Show him in!

PICKEL (*entering*): Excuse me, good man, you don't have to handle me so roughly. Who are you, anyway? You know, you live in a big city with all the rabble, but you ought to be able to distinguish between me and them...

COMMISSIONER: What's your name?

PICKEL: I have come from Holzhausen, which is in the principality of Münsing, which—

COMMISSIONER: Did you hear my question?

PICKEL: Well now, I was just saying that I have come—

COMMISSIONER: What is your name?

PICKEL: Pickel. Born in Holzhausen, Wetzlar Circle.

COMMISSIONER: You were in the room with the Minister shortly before the attack. What did you want there?

PICKEL: Now look here, fine Sir, it's important you hear this. I thought the Minister was an honorable man. I voted for him, and would have done so again. I'm not a political person, by any means, no axe to grind here. But when I came to visit him in his hotel room—

COMMISSIONER: You admit, then, that you had a personal reason to kill the Minister?

PICKEL: Well, you see, like I said, I always thought the Minister was an honorable man. But after I saw him earlier that day at the Ministry—

COMMISSIONER: Are you an anarchist? Do you belong to any secret societies?

PICKEL: Indeed, I am a member of a Veterans' Association. And also a Masonic Lodge.

COMMISSIONER: Ooooh…. (*To ASSISTANT*) Write that down, Veterans' Association and Freemasonry! Can you prove this?

PICKEL: Of course, General. Here are my membership cards. (*Searches through his pockets.*) Now where are they—

COMMISSIONER: Were you a soldier?

PICKEL: Of course.

COMMISSIONER: At the front.

PICKEL: No, in the rear. On the telephone. On account of the logjam—

COMMISSIONER: Never mind. Please just tell me the order of the events.

PICKEL: Certainly—so first I must ask you, do you know of Holzhausen? West of Degerndorf? I came here from Holzhausen because of the railroad.—I didn't come on the railroad, I hate railroads! That is, I came on the mail-coach—I wanted to speak to the Prime Minister and so I went to the Ministry. (*COMMISSIONER waits*) That's it. There's nothing more to add.

COMMISSIONER: That's all you have to say.

PICKEL: Well, I could say more, of course, if you want me to. The weather's gotten better, it's not raining anymore. My wife always tells me—

COMMISSIONER: Please, stop talking. (*To ASSISTANT*) This man is an idiot. Take his particulars, and document all his belongings.

ASSISTANT: Your name? First and last.

PICKEL: My name is Traugott Pickel. As a boy I was called Gottlieb, but my real name is Traugott. I was named by the official at the Registry Office who was my father's cousin, they used to play cards every night—

COMMISSIONER (*grabs his notebook*): Take off your coat.

PICKEL: But I'm wearing it.

COMMISSIONER: Come on! Off with the frock!

(*The door flies open, THOMAS standing, with the POLICEMEN*)

COMMISSIONER (*seeing him*): A waiter's uniform!

POLICEMAN 1: We found this man in the city park. He had a revolver in his hand. Two bullets missing.

COMMISSIONER: Your name?

THOMAS: Karl Thomas.

COMMISSIONER: What were you doing with this gun?

THOMAS: I was going to shoot the Minister.

COMMISSIONER: Did you hear that? A confession! Do you belong to the Veterans' Association along with Pickel here?

PICKEL: General, our Veterans' Association doesn't take members from other towns. Only the President of the Reich!

COMMISSIONER: Shut up!

PICKEL: —is an honorary member.

COMMISSIONER: So. Why did you shoot him?

THOMAS: I didn't shoot him.

COMMISSIONER: But you've just confessed.

PICKEL: You are mistaken, General. I know this man. He is a close friend of the Minister's—

COMMISSIONER: I'll have you locked up if you're not quiet! (*to THOMAS*) You saw the Minister as a threat, yes? A traitor to the nation?

THOMAS: The murderer certainly thought he was.

COMMISSIONER: The murderer?

THOMAS: The one who shot Kilman. I ran after him, I shot at him. Twice.

COMMISSIONER: What madness are you saying now?

ASSISTANT (*crosses to COMMISSIONER*): He made no attempt to hide the gun. (*Touches his head.*)

COMMISSIONER: I had the same thought! We'll discharge him to the doctor. (*On the telephone*) Connect me to the Public Prosecutor—

PICKEL: Commissioner—

COMMISSIONER: Silence. I'll throw you in jail for disorderly conduct if you say one more word.

PICKEL: Then I'll be a criminal! A disgrace! I can never show my face in Holzhausen again. What will my wife say? And my neighbor... and the friend of my father's at the Registry... and everyone in the Veterans' Association...

COMMISSIONER: Shut up! If your account is verified, you are free to go.

PICKEL: Now one has to have their innocence proven! White gloves, black gloves. What is one supposed to believe?

(*Blackout*)

Scene Three. Courtroom

COURT ROOM. *JUDGE presiding.*

KARL THOMAS handcuffed, standing in front of the table.

JUDGE: You're only making your case worse. There are eye-witnesses who testify that you swore to murder the Prime Minister.

THOMAS: I don't deny that. But I did not shoot him.

JUDGE: Then you admit to intent?

THOMAS: Intent, yes.

JUDGE: Calling Witness Rand. (*RAND enters*) Mr. Rand, do you know the accused?

RAND: Yes, your Honor.

JUDGE: Is this the same man who stole your revolver during the riot at the polling station?

RAND: Yes, your Honor.

JUDGE: What do you say to that, Thomas?

THOMAS: I don't deny it.

RAND: Karl Thomas is innocent.

JUDGE: Oh, really?

RAND: Yes. It's my personal belief that the Jews are behind it.

JUDGE (*ignoring this*): Had you shot this revolver at the time, Mr. Rand?

RAND: No, your Honor. It should have all the bullets present and accounted for.

JUDGE: It is missing two. And is that your revolver?

RAND: Yes, that is my service revolver, your Honor.

JUDGE: Do you still deny that you did the deed, Thomas?

THOMAS: I have nothing to confess.

JUDGE: How do you explain the absence of two bullets, then?

THOMAS: I fired at the murderer.

JUDGE: So, you fired at the murderer. Well, this Great Unknown Assassin is nowhere to be found. Who was this mysterious person, who entered the room and shot the Prime Minister?

THOMAS: A right-wing fanatic. He said so himself. I ran after him. I thought he would be a comrade in the struggle.

JUDGE: Everyone knows that revolutionary violence comes from the left, not the right. Do you think you can cover the tracks of your confederates? We have a record of you, Karl Thomas, and this time there will be no amnesty. The court calls on the woman known as Mother Meller. (*MOTHER MELLER enters*) Do you know the accused?

MELLER: Yes. He is my friend.

JUDGE: Your friend. You might call him your comrade?

MELLER: Yes, I have called him that.

JUDGE: And you helped the accused find work at the Grand Hotel?

MELLER (*bows her head, with difficulty*): I did.

JUDGE: You stand accused of aiding and abetting a political assassin. Pull yourself together.

MELLER: If you know the answers already, why are you questioning me?

JUDGE: Did the accused say, quote, "You're all asleep! You need a shot to wake you all up!"?

MELLER: No, I don't recall him saying that.

JUDGE: The court calls the Page at the Hotel to the stand. (*PAGE enters, with Head-Waiter.*) Do you know the accused?

PAGE: Yes, your Honor. When he was carrying plates, he dropped one and broke one and told me to hide the pieces so they wouldn't find it.

JUDGE: We're not interested in that at the moment. Now listen carefully to me. Did you hear the accused say: "You are all asleep! Someone must be taken out. Then you will all wake up"?

PAGE (*sounding rehearsed*): Yes, your Honor. He had blood-shot eyes and clenched his fists when he said it. He looked like someone I've only seen in the movies. I was so scared.

JUDGE: Where did you go then?

PAGE: I—I—

JUDGE: Remember, you are sworn to tell the truth.

PAGE (*turns away from the JUDGE to the HEAD-WAITER*): Sir, I don't want to do this anymore. I told you, I wanted to leave. I was tired, I hid under the table and tried to get a little sleep.—Sir, please don't report me to the Manager—

JUDGE (*laughing*): The witnesses can go. Please arrest Mrs. Meller and bring in Albert Kroll. (*WITNESSES go; ALBERT KROLL enters.*) Is your name Albert Kroll?

ALBERT: Yes.

JUDGE: Do you know the accused?

ALBERT: I know him, and I think this is a joke. Thomas may be excitable, but there is a great difference between thinking something and doing it.

THOMAS: I'm not as weak as you think I am, Albert.

JUDGE: You are being held, Mr. Kroll, on the suspicion of being one of the intellectual authors of the murder. (*ALBERT KROLL laughs.*) You should stop laughing, if you know what's good for you.

ALBERT: Do you think we're idiots? Do you think, if Kilman were murdered, that the whole rotten system would collapse along with him?

JUDGE: You were talking of it, openly, to workers, at assemblies.

ALBERT: It's a pity you steer clear of our meetings, Mr. Judge. You could learn a few things.

JUDGE: You admit, then, that you saw Kilman as a traitor to your cause?

ALBERT: If by traitor you mean someone who betrays the cause, out of greed or evil? No. Kilman genuinely believed that his tactics were the right ones, that he was a "minister of the people." He couldn't have foreseen that they would result in his own death and in the continued death of our democracy. But I'm not going to debate politics with you. You must have other "assassins" that you need to question.

THOMAS: He was killed by the right! I already told them, Albert, but they don't believe me.

JUDGE: Why would someone on the right have shot him?

ALBERT: Kilman was no longer one of us, but he also wasn't one of them. For the right, even a moderate like Kilman deserves to be shot.

JUDGE: Lead him away. Bring in the prisoner Eva Berg. (*EVA BERG enters.*) Your name is Eva Berg?

EVA BERG (*not answering or looking at him*): Hello, Karl.

JUDGE: You are not allowed to speak to the accused.

EVA: You'll fool them all, won't you, Karl?

JUDGE: I'll have you held in contempt if you don't change your tone.

EVA: You hide behind the law. I've been in prison for weeks already. I have rights, granted to me by the constitution.

JUDGE: I have two questions, then you can go. Did the accused ever live with you?

EVA: Yes.

JUDGE: Did the two of you have an unlawful relationship?

EVA: What kind of a question is that?

JUDGE: Did you engage in sexual relations with the accused?

EVA: Would you tell me first what un-sexual relations look like?

JUDGE: You come from a good family. Your father—

EVA: My family isn't worth a damn to you. And I am ashamed to answer your prurient questions.

JUDGE: You refuse to answer, let the record show. My second question: Did the accused, while he was living with you, express his desire to murder Minister Kilman?

EVA: This question is as ludicrous as your others, but I swear that Karl Thomas never once expressed a desire to murder Kilman.

JUDGE: Thank you. Lead her away.

EVA: Goodbye, Karl. Don't let them get to you.

THOMAS: I love you, Eva.

EVA (*looks at him with disgust, sighs*): You really shouldn't say such stupid things. (*EVA BERG is led away.*)

JUDGE (*turns to KARL THOMAS*): According to your files, you spent eight years in a madhouse. In order to establish your criminal liability, you will be referred to the Department of Psychiatry.

(*Blackout*)

Scene Four. Madhouse

MADHOUSE. EXAMINATION ROOM.
(*The same setting as Scene Two*).

PROFESSOR LÜDIN: Tell me, honestly, why did you do it?

THOMAS: I didn't.

PROFESSOR: You can trust me. I'm only interested in your motives.

THOMAS: How can I confess if I did not do it?

PROFESSOR: You sought revenge, didn't you? You felt betrayed.

THOMAS: You will torture me until I truly go mad, won't you?

PROFESSOR: Very suspicious. (*KARL THOMAS laughs.*) Don't laugh, please. Now tell me why you shot him.

THOMAS: I remember—I remember the door slamming shut behind me, and leaving this madhouse after eight long years. First thing I did, just as you recommended, I went to see Kilman at the Ministry. He had been sentenced to death, just like me, eight years ago. And I saw him sitting there, Minister of the Interior, sipping cocktails with all the enemies from our past.

PROFESSOR: Perfectly normal. Just smarter than you.

THOMAS: I went to my best comrades, Eva Berg and Albert Kroll. Once, I saw them beat back an entire battalion with revolvers in their hands. And now, I heard them tell me: "You need to find work. You should learn how to wait tables."

PROFESSOR: Normal.

THOMAS: So I became a waiter. For one evening, I worked with another former comrade in the bowels of the Grand Hotel. It stank of corruption, lust, and filth. My coworkers, they all thought it was normal!

PROFESSOR: And it is normal. The economy is blooming again. Full employment. Everyone earns money their own way.

THOMAS: I thought up a plan for all humanity. I found a revolver. I wanted to shoot him, Kilman, the Minister. But before I had a chance, someone else did. I asked the murderer, thinking he was my comrade, why? And I heard the sound of his voice. "Because he was a Bolshevik," he whispered to me. "A revolutionary." Selling our country to the Jews.

PROFESSOR: Normal. Or, it would be, if this person actually existed, and wasn't just a figment of your imagination.

THOMAS: I wanted to end it all. I wanted to shoot myself. Maybe the world isn't so crazy after all. Maybe it's me—maybe I am the one who isn't normal—

PROFESSOR: On the contrary. Your logical faculties seem to be functioning.

THOMAS: But there's a murderer out there, running loose, a criminal!

PROFESSOR: Let's assume you're speaking the truth, that you really did want to "wake up" mankind by doing this foolish thing. Wake them up to what, my friend? If the world wanted everyone to dine equally, there would be no poverty.

THOMAS: Stop! You're making my head hurt. (*Starts laughing*) It's madness! Madness!

PROFESSOR: Hey, we're not acting in a comedy here.

THOMAS: All of us must be cured! And you first!

PROFESSOR: Don't be a fool. Here, I'll show you what it really looks like to be crazy in the world. Look at the screen. Here you will see a banker who thinks he can control the stock exchange and become the richest man in the world. Little does he know, he's just a random victim!

PROJECTION: Private Room, Hotel

BANKER (*on the telephone*): Hello? Hello! Stock exchange? Sell! Sell! Everything! Colors, potassium, rubies—Kilman's been shot—factory shares have fallen 100 percent—what?—Hello?—(*Dials frantically*) Operator! Operator! Why did you disconnect me?—I'll hold you liable for this, you—ruined by telephone trouble—God in heaven!

THOMAS: I saw him, in the flesh, just last night at the hotel. He told me he brings in enough money to burn it—and what use is it to him? He can't even fill his belly with delicacies. As the others dined on pheasant, he was spooning broth because his stomach was too soft. Day and night he speculates. Why? What's the reason? Hahaha!

PROFESSOR: Perfectly normal! Wish there were more like him! At least he's trying to make something of himself!

BANKER (*grinning, in the Hotel room, falls on his knees, takes out a gun, holds it to his head*): I'm ruined!—But this is entirely normal... normal... normal... (*blackout*).

PROFESSOR: And the porter at the Grand Hotel, who's lost his mind due to hyperinflation. Saved 700 million and couldn't even buy a box of matches. He has slowly gone insane, settling up and reckoning accounts with paper money, and today he saves the crumbs that fall from his mouth and gambles his last penny on horses.

PROJECTION: Servants' Room

PORTER: Who won at the Paris races? The beautiful Galatea—Shit! It's all a racket! I put all my savings on Idealist, and the goddamned Jockey goes and breaks his neck—I want my stake back!

THOMAS: He saved for twelve years. And then the inflation came. Hahaha!

PROFESSOR: Suffers from paralysis of the brain. Nothing wagered, nothing won! The porter at the Grand Hotel—I've lodged there myself—is utterly normal, typical of her kind.

PORTER (*stabs himself with a knife, grinning*): normal... normal... (*blackout*).

PROFESSOR: Next! An inventor of an apparatus which could help all the people in the world. But the apparatus was destroyed by an investor. Because it wouldn't make him enough money!

PROJECTION: Radio Station

OPERATOR: Attention! Attention! All radio stations of the world. Who will buy my invention? I don't want money, I just want to help everyone.—Hello? Hello?—No response…

THOMAS: The telegram operator. Wanted to sell her patent because it creates peace and not war. You call this a normal world, destroying the most important inventions, because they make people's lives better and don't make money!? Hahaha!

OPERATOR (*making a short circuit, grinning*): Normal… normal… normal…

PROFESSOR: Suffers from paranoia, and a madwoman to boot. An inventor who imagines they've invented an apparatus able to nourish all the hungry by distilling sugar from wood. Just like Jehovah. But the apparatus has been destroyed by a sugar investor. Life is not a peaceful meadow, Karl Thomas. Life is a struggle. He who has the strongest fists wins. All absolutely normal. And the last! An innocent, formerly a chauffeur, but now unexpectedly in the driver's seat. He's deluded by the idea that he's the motor driving the automobile, when in fact he's only the horn, making loud and insignificant noises!

(*On the façade of the madhouse, where the Hotel was located, a mad scene. The mask of KILMAN, distorted in madness*)

KILMAN: The text of my regulations will prevent any recession. A milestone of progress. Print up this speech! I'm proud of it. (*Grinning*) Normal… normal… normal…

THOMAS: Ah, yes, Minister Kilman. But I thought you were dead!

PROFESSOR: Don't mock his sacrifice, Karl Thomas! Prudence in a time of trouble.

THOMAS (*hallucinating, speaking to the MASK of PROFESSOR LÜDIN*): Can you tell me? What does it mean to be normal? And what does it mean to be mad?

PROFESSOR: Who are you talking to now?

THOMAS (*speaking to the MASK, hallucination continuing*): Don't tell me that you, too, are normal—please, I'm waiting for your answer! Normal... normal... normal! (*MASK disappears.*)

PROFESSOR: Now you're speaking to figments, Thomas, to thin air. You should have just confessed.

THOMAS: I'm such a fool! I see it all clearly now. They've transformed the world into a madhouse. There's no difference being in here and being outside. Back in those days, we marched together, under the flag of paradise. But now—one must put one's boots on the ground.—You trust, you live—it drives you to the abyss. You are just one man. You can't do a thing! The world remains as it always has. (*KARL THOMAS, hallucinating once again, now hears the sound of boots marching outside.*)

CHORUS OUTSIDE (*from a whisper to a shout*): Karl Thomas! Karl Thomas!

PROFESSOR (*to the GUARDS*): What is that?

GUARD (*At the window*): A demonstration. For the prisoner.

CHORUS OUTSIDE: Hooray for Karl Thomas! Hooray for Karl Thomas! (*On the street, cinematically visible, an incalculable, silent train of demonstrating humanity.*)

PROFESSOR: It's all beginning, all over again. You've done it with your mad deed!

THOMAS: I have?

PROFESSOR: Yes! Don't be such a hypocrite!

THOMAS: But I haven't done anything. (*Short pause*) I haven't done a thing! (*Suddenly KARL THOMAS laughs, a horrible, whinnying, uncontrollable sound.*)

PROFESSOR: Don't laugh. That won't save you.

THOMAS (*laughs*).

PROFESSOR: Incurably insane.

THOMAS (*laughs*).

PROFESSOR (*stops in front of Karl Thomas, considers him for a moment*): A seizure. He really is crazy. Take him to the isolation ward. Buchenwald. (*KARL THOMAS is led away by the guards.*) A sad case, this. Incurable. Unable to survive life. (*As the people march out in silence, the curtain closes.*)

TITLE CARD: This was the original ending written by Ernst Toller in 1927. However, Erwin Piscator—the play's director—demanded a new ending that was more politically "objective."

New Ending

SCENE: THE HOTEL: The BANKER, PORTER, and OPERATOR are visible. All repeating the word "Normal... normal... normal..." Explosion in the Hotel. Blackout.

THOMAS: I'm such a fool! They've transformed the world into a madhouse. There's no difference being in here and being outside. I see it all so clearly now.

PROFESSOR: Life is struggle. The strongest wins. All perfectly normal.

THOMAS: But that's madness! How come you get to say what is and isn't "normal"? You are the real madman! Just imagine—the world remaining forever as it is just now!

PROFESSOR: If everyone shared your insane ideas, Karl Thomas, nobody would go to work in the morning. Do you think that all who are hungry deserve to eat? If nature wanted us to eat less, there would be no poverty.

THOMAS: What, then? You want everyone to remain miserable, poor, and starving? Are you happy?

PROFESSOR: What is "happiness"! An idea. A concept that's all in your head. What do you want? To uproot life by its foundations? To create heaven on earth? To uplift the masses?

THOMAS: What do you know about the masses?

PROFESSOR: The masses are a herd of pigs. They belly up to feed at the trough, then wallow in the mud and shit when their bellies are full. And every century, some new psychopath like you comes along to proclaim a new paradise for the herd. If you want to hold onto this romantic idea, this myth, go ahead. But please, I beg you. Write poetry. Join a religious sect. But no! You have to go and try to make the world "a better place." We're better off without lunatics like you.

THOMAS: Go to hell.

PROFESSOR: It's my mission to protect society from dangerous, antisocial criminals like you. You must be sterilized, rendered harmless, euthanized, eliminated!

THOMAS: Guard! Guard! (*GUARDS enter.*) Lock this madman up in an isolation cell! (*GUARDS grab KARL THOMAS.*) He's a criminal, I'm telling you!

PROFESSOR: In the morning you will be transported back to prison. Normal, normal... (*Curtain.*)

ACT FIVE

Scene One

PRISON. *For a moment, all cells are visible. Then blackout.*

ALBERT KROLL's CELL.

ALBERT KROLL: Who's there?

EVA BERG: Eva.

ALBERT: You too.

EVA: Earlier today.

ALBERT: And the others?

EVA: All arrested. Why did Karl do it?

ALBERT: He says he didn't. Where is he?

EVA: Maybe Mother Meller knows.

ALBERT: Mother Meller? She's here too?

EVA: Yes. Right above me. Wait, I'll knock.

(*Noise at ALBERT KROLL's door.*)

ALBERT: Wait! Someone's Coming.

(*Cell door screeches open. Enter RAND.*)

RAND: Soup. Eat it quick.

ALBERT: Oh, it's you.

RAND: Yes, we're all together again. All except Kilman, of course. They're unveiling his memorial today.

ALBERT: Really?

RAND: You have to admit, he was the only one of you who was good for anything.

ALBERT: Tell me, where is Karl Thomas?

RAND: I can't tell you. That guy—what a life he's got behind him... (*Exits.*)

ALBERT: Psst. Eva.

EVA: Where is Karl?

KARL THOMAS'S CELL

KARL THOMAS: Who's there?

MOTHER MELLER: Mother Meller.

THOMAS: What? You in prison? Who else is here?

MELLER: We're all here. Eva. Albert. Just like eight years ago. Although now we're locked up in separate cells. I can't understand why you've done what you've done, Karl, but I want you to know: I'll stand by you.

THOMAS: Listen! Who's that?

PRISONER N'S CELL

PRISONER N: Not so loud. You'll get us in trouble.

THOMAS (*knocks*): Who are you?

PRISONER N (*knocks*): If you keep this up, there's no hope
for us... I won't answer you any more... (*blackout*).

THOMAS: Ah, it's you!—I thought you were dead—all of us
here again—can it be? Is it possible?—The dance begins
again?—Still waiting, waiting, waiting—what allows one
to go on?—No one listens—we speak and we never hear
ourselves—we murder and we never feel ourselves—must
it always be this way?—Will I ever understand you?—Will
you ever understand me?—Never! Never! Never!—Who
are you who smash, burn, gas the entire earth?—For no
reason at all?—From the highest mountain—from the
highest tree—the flood—(*KARL THOMAS tears off a strip
of his bedsheet, climbs up on the stool, and fastens the
strip to the door-hook. Blackout in his cell.*)

GROUP standing in front of a veiled monument.
COUNT LANDE speaking.

COUNT: And so I commend unto the people, the monument of
this deserving man, who in difficult times— (*blackout as
he keeps speaking.*)

ALBERT KROLL'S CELL

(*Noises. Door screeches open. Enter RAND*)

RAND: The Ministry of Justice just called, and Thomas isn't the murderer. They caught the real one in Switzerland. A student. As he was being arrested, he shot himself.

ALBERT: Will they let us go?

RAND: Not today. Today is Sunday. But congratulations, Mr. Kroll. I hope the best for you. (*Exits.*)

ALBERT (*as he knocks, FILM crawl at the front of the stage*): "Thomas is not the murderer, they have the others."

(*Bottom left*): "Thomas is not the murderer."

(*Bottom right*): "We are all free. Karl, my dear boy, you've got a shot after all. They have the murderer.

(*All the other PRISONERS knock*) Karl… Karl… Karl…"

(*Silence*)

"He does not answer."

"He does not answer." (*Knocking throughout the Prison.*)

(*Silence*)

TITLE CARD: This is ending number 2. Karl Thomas back in prison, committing suicide with none of his fellow comrades learning what has happened. Piscator didn't demand a rewrite this time. Instead, on opening night, he simply wrote a new, final ending himself.

RAND (*screams*): He's hanged himself!

MELLER: Is it true?

KROLL: He wasn't allowed to do that. No revolutionary dies like that!

EVA: Everyday life has broken him.

MELLER: Damned world!—It must be changed.

END OF PLAY

About Ernst Toller

ERNST TOLLER was a revolutionary, poet, and playwright, as well as President of the short-lived Bavarian Soviet Republic. He was born in 1893 in Posen, now Poznań (Poland). In 1914, like many young patriotic Germans, Toller enlisted in the Kaiser's army. Instead of glorious victory, he saw the horrors of trench warfare. Wounded at the front, he suffered a complete physical and psychological collapse.

He consequently embraced revolutionary socialism and joined the leadership of the Bavarian Soviet Republic. For six days, in April of 1919, Toller served as President in Munich and head of the Bavarian Soviet army. Right-wing paramilitary troupes and the Bavarian army easily quashed the revolution. Lucky to escape with his life, Toller stood trial on charges of treason and was sentenced to five years in prison.

While incarcerated in Niederschönenfeld Prison, Toller began writing poems and plays drawing on his experience. From 1920 to 1925, unable to attend the premieres of his plays, he spoke for an entire generation. He was the *Arbeiterdichter*, "Workers' Poet". At a time when Bert Brecht was still virtually unknown, Toller was the most high-profile playwright of the German left, his name synonymous with the avant-garde and political commitment.

Following his release, he searched for a new direction. The poet who still remembered a world in the frenzy of revolution encountered a teeming urban chaos in thrall to the distractions of capitalism.

Toller's following alliance with *Volksbühne* director Erwin

Piscator was a natural one. Piscator's own politicized productions, inflected with Dadaist revolt, Bauhaus aesthetics, and Soviet agitprop, had electrified audiences and outraged critics. When Piscator was fired, Toller pledged his support. He accused the *Volksbühne*, the "People's Theater," of betraying its mission and the two men discussed creating a magazine together before starting work on *Hoppla! We're Alive!*

Toller's Jewish ancestry, leftism, and avant-gardism made him a prime target for discrimination once the Nazis came to power. In 1933, the Nazi party placed Toller on a list of "undesirable" writers. His books were burned. Toller fled to London before a lecture tour took him to the United States. Eventually settling in New York City, he joined a group of like-minded literary emigres and writers in exile, including Klaus and Erika Mann, the children of Thomas Mann.

On December 24, 1938, Piscator sailed from Paris to America. The New School had established the *Dramatic Workshop*, which Piscator would direct and which would serve as a home for many German artists in exile. Early the following spring, Piscator met with Toller in the Mayflower Hotel on Central Park West. He found him depressed, unable to find work, once more a man imprisoned by circumstance.

Toller had also just learned that his brother and sister had been sent to a concentration camp. On top of this, his marriage to Christine Grautoff was falling apart. He had been involved in raising funds, giving speeches, and rallying the world's attention to support Republican fighters in the Spanish Civil War, only for Franco's forces to defeat the Republicans. Two weeks later, on May 22, 1939, Toller was found dead by hanging, a presumed suicide, in his room at the Mayflower Hotel.

In 1965, Piscator wrote that Toller had made clear that it was "life—or rather, the times—whose dramaturgy he felt imprisoned him, and that he could only escape their inexorable consequences by writing a horrible ending, once and for all."

Photo: *National Library of Israel, Schwadron collection*

About The Play

In summer 1926, Ernst Toller traveled to the Baltic coast with Erwin Piscator. The result of this collaboration was *Hoppla, wir leben! (Hoppla, We're Alive!)*. The philosopher Peter Sloterdijk has hailed it as "one of the most impressive plays of the decade, saturated with the experience of the era and marked by the bitterest of growing-pains, but clear-eyed in its realism."

Hoppla! premiered September 3, 1927 at Piscator's new venture, the Piscatorbühne at Berlin's Theater am Nollendorfplatz. It would revolutionize the modern theater. Piscator objected to Toller's *dichterische Lyrik,* "poetic lyricism ", and debts to Expressionism. Characteristically, the director altered the text in rehearsals. He cut Toller's lyrical, poetic speeches and inserted filmic montages of documentary materials. He used projections as title cards, introducing and interrupting scenes. He added a cabaret-style song with lyrics by Walter Mehring, music by Edmund Meisel, and choreography by Kate Kühl. The play itself was staged on designer Traugott Müller's enormous set, consisting of multi-level steel scaffolding. This enabled him to change locations and cut between scenes with sudden changes of light and sound. Piscator's radical style, as of then unnamed, is now known as epic theater. (After *Hoppla!* premiered, Brecht would work at the *Piscatorbühne* as a dramaturg.)

The English-language version seen here premiered, with some cuts, at La Mama Experimental Theater Club in 2019, directed by Zishan Ugurlu. This was the New York premiere of the play—no prior record of its performance has been found. For this edition, the translator has restored those passages, that reflect the scope of Piscator and Toller's collaboration. He consulted Toller's four-act typewritten manuscript from 1926, the unpublished *Lotz Manuscript* of 1927, the Kiepenheuer Verlag version, and Piscator's director's *Regiebuch* "promptbook", in Berlin's Akademie der Künste.

About Drew Lichtenberg

DREW LICHTENBERG is a writer, translator, teacher, and dramaturg. He was born in Philadelphia into a theatrical family. His parents met as graduate students at the University of Massachusetts-Amherst. At the time he was born, his father was running the education department and directing plays at Philadelphia's Walnut Street Theatre. His mother received her Masters of Fine Art in Dramaturgy in Amherst, MA. He followed in her footsteps, making him one of the few multi-generational dramaturgs in America, where the field is younger than in European theater.

Lichtenberg became fascinated by German Expressionism and the theater of the Weimer Republic as an undergraduate already. In 2018, he completed his doctorate at the Yale School of Drama. His thesis was a dramaturgical reconstruction of the Piscatorbühne season of 1927-28.

Lichtenberg currently lives in Washington, D.C., where he has been the dramaturg in residence at the Shakespeare Theatre Company for more than ten years. He has worked at stages such as the Royal National Theatre in London, the Roundabout Theatre on Broadway, and the Brooklyn Academy of Music and the Public Theater off-Broadway. He has also taught courses at Yale, the New School, and the Catholic University of America. Routledge published his monography, *The Piscatorbühne Century: Aesthetics and Politics in the Modern Theatre,* in 2021. He is the life partner of Rebecca Ende Lichtenberg and proud parent of Dylan and Noah Lichtenberg.

Photo: Teresa Wood

Presents

Sign up for our
Newsletter at
berlinica.com

Writers from Berlin
Our West-Berlin
Softcover; $19.95, 224 pages
6x9"; 65 pictures b/w
ISBN: 978-1-935902-54-6

Alexander Roda Roda
Springtime in America
Softcover; $12.95,136 pages
Dimensions: 5.5x8.5"
ISBN: 978-1-935902-01-0

Ernst Toller
Hinkemann. A Tragedy
Softcover; $11.95, 86 pages
Dimensions: 5x8"
ISBN: 978-1-935902-52-2

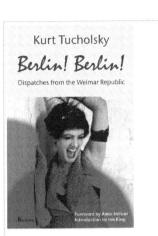

Kurt Tucholsky
Berlin! Berlin!
Softcover; $14.00, 208 pages
5.5x8.5", 41 pictures b/w
ISBN: 978-3-960260-27-1

Kurt Tucholsky
Germany? Germany!
Softcover; $15.00, 208 pages
5.5x8.5", 6 b/w pictures
ISBN: 978-1-935902-38-9

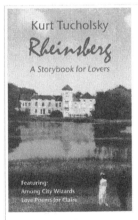

Kurt Tucholsky
Rheinsberg
Hardcover; $12.95, 96 pages
5x8", 26 pictures color & bw
ISBN: 978-1-935902-25-6

Kurt Tucholsky
Hereafter
Hardcover; $12.95, 96 pages
5x8", 23 color pictures
ISBN: 978-1-935902-89-8

Harold Poor
Kurt Tucholsky
Softcover; $19.95, 256 pages
6x9", 21 pictures b/w
ISBN: 978-1-935902-47-8

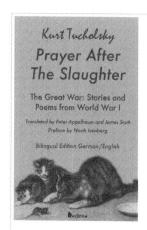

Kurt Tucholsky
Prayer After The Slaughter
Softcover; $12.95, 116 pages
5x8", 6 b/w pictures
ISBN: 978-1-935902-28-7

Donna Swarthout
A Place They Called Home
Hardcover; $19.95, 208 pages
6x9", 12 pictures b/w
ISBN: 978-1-935902-65-2

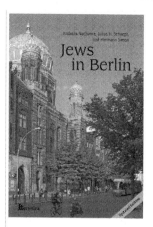

Nachama, Schoeps, Simon
Jews in Berlin
Softcover; $26.95, 310 pages
6x9", 372 pictures b/w & color
ISBN: 978-1-935902-60-7

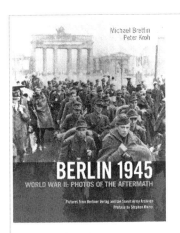

Michael Brettin
Berlin 1945
Softcover; $24.95, 218 pages
8.5x11", 177 pictures b/w
ISBN: 978-1-935902-02-7

Andreas Austilat
Mark Twain in Berlin
Softcover; $13.95, 176 pages
5.5x8.5", 68 pictures b/w
ISBN: 978-1-935902-95-9

Michael Cramer
The Berlin Wall Today
Softcover, $15.95, 102 pages
8.5x8.5"; 174 pics/maps full color
ISBN: 978-1-935902-10-2

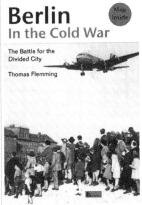

Thomas Flemming
Berlin in the Cold War
Softcover, $10.95, 90 pages
6.7x9.5"; 54 pics & maps b/w
ISBN: 978-1-935902-80-5

Rose Marie Donhauser
The Berlin Cookbook
Softcover, $15.00, 104 pages
8.5x8.5"; 60 Recipes
ISBN: 978-3-960260-5-47

Lothar Heinke
Wings of Desire
Softcover; $16.95, 102 pages
7.5x9.25", 123 pictures full color
ISBN: 978-1-935902-14-0

Sebastian Ringel
Leipzig!
Softcover; $24.95, 224 pages
6.7x9.5", 224 pictures b/w & color
ISBN: 978-1-935902-59-1

Cornelia Dömer
Martin Luther's Travel Guide
Softcover; $13.95, 176 pages
5x8", 140 full color pics & maps
ISBN: 978-1-935902-44-7